Earn $300 a Day Mowing Lawns

A Complete Beginner's Guide to the Lawn Mowing Business

James T. Adams

Adams Mowing

Toledo, Ohio

ccp

Published by Crane Creek Press

Toledo, Ohio

www.cranecreekpress.com

cranecreekpress@gmail.com

ISBN: 978-0-9886099-0-7

Quick Start Guide

In a hurry? Follow the steps below and you can start earning mowing money in a matter of days.

Read the first five chapters of this book.

Advertise. Call local newspapers and place classified ads as described in Chapter 3. Be sure your ads will run in older neighborhoods with small lawns.

Keep it legal, part one. Call your insurance agent and obtain insurance coverages required in your locality. (See Chapter 2.)

Keep it legal, part two. Check the phone book and call state and local government information offices to see if licenses or permits are required. (See Chapter 2.)

Equipment. You will need some sort of mower, some sort of trimmer, and a broom. These may be new or used, and they may be owned, borrowed, rented, or bought, possibly at a garage sale or a second-hand store.

Go to work. When prospects call, estimate jobs as described in Chapter 4 and mow them as described in Chapter 5. At this early stage, collect your money as you complete each job.

Contents

Introduction

The purpose of this guidebook is to show you how to earn at least $300 a day mowing lawns. Over twenty-odd years in business I've earned that much and more in two different ways.

One is with a crew-type operation. This is the standard outfit you see all the time: sizeable truck, several crew members, and a large trailer carrying maybe ten assorted turf machines — mowers, blowers, tractors, edgers, etc.

This massive, expensive rig can definitely net $300 a day. But because of inherent inefficiencies and high overhead expenses, you'll have to cut upwards of $1,000 worth of grass to do it. That's like having a real job. Make that two real jobs.

You can also earn $300 a day with a much smaller rig. Typically, this is a one-person operation, with a small truck and trailer carrying a large, powerful commercial mowing tractor and little else. When I first started operating this way, in the early 1990s, I seemed to be alone. Today, I see a few such rigs, but not many.

The emphasis with this smaller rig is on efficiency — efficiency far beyond what is possible with a crew. I call it high-efficiency lawn mowing. By operating at extremely high levels of efficiency while holding expenses down, you can earn $300 by cutting about $400 worth of grass. Which is to say, compared to a crew, you'll earn the same money by doing less than half the work. If nothing else, that's pretty cool. A high-efficiency set up also allows you to retain much of that independent, take-this-job-and-shove-it attitude that steers many of us to the mowing business in the first place.

Both approaches are discussed at length in the chapters ahead.

How quickly you reach $300 a day — or whether you reach it at all — is a different question. In the end, success in the lawn mowing business doesn't come from plans, or schemes, or heaps of start-up cash, or connections, or advertising skills, or a gift of gab, or any such stuff. Lots of beginners think these things are important, but over the long haul they mean little. Over the years, I've seen many people with such apparent advantages fall flat on their faces.

Success depends chiefly upon two factors: First, your ability to attract and hold customers. If you don't learn how to create customer loyalty, you'll always be starting over, and never build up enough sales volume to worry about. And second, your ability to operate efficiently. If you don't operate efficiently, money comes in but goes right back out in the form of expenses. You can mow every blade of grass in Texas and never make a dime.

These two factors — creating satisfied customers and operating efficiently — are the central themes of this guide. I return to them repeatedly, examining them in depth from various angles. I hope you will give them close attention. Learn to do these two things well, and the lawn mowing business will be very, very good to you. I guarantee it.

Jim Adams

1. Management

To manage a business is to make decisions. There's really nothing more to it than that. What services to offer; how much to charge for them; how, when, and where to advertise; how to deal with customers; who to hire or fire; policies on buying, bidding, scheduling, setting work rules and quality standards — these and a thousand other decisions are yours to make. When you are running a business, the ball is always in your court.

In the mowing business, all you have to do to succeed is make fairly good choices. This isn't rocket science — perfection is not required. If you don't know it already, you'll soon discover that there are a whole lot of dummies out there among your competitors. They make every mistake imaginable ... lots of them are self-employed because they can't (or won't) hold even a burger-flipping job. That means you never have to go head-to-head with big, fancy, well-heeled outfits. Just be a little smarter than the dummies, and everything will work fine.

This chapter is about making those smarter choices. I discuss major issues, perhaps adding a little background information. Then I give you my opinion of what you should do. We might not agree. Our life experiences and goals are different, and so may be our choices. But at least you'll know what I think and why.

Entering the Market

From the outside, the market for a given service — mowing, window washing, parking-lot sweeping —

might appear to be sewed up. At first glance it looks like one big company "owns" all three upscale malls, another outfit "owns" most of the fancy apartment complexes, etc. So it appears, always, everywhere. From the outside, the gaps and holes are not apparent.

They are there, nevertheless. Those big outfits that seem to own the market have their own Achilles' heel, in the form of big expenses. They pay for such things as workers, mechanics, secretaries, managers, buildings, and much more. To pay these expenses, they have to charge high prices. In the process, they price themselves out of a large part of the market.

As a raw beginner, where do you start? How do you break into the marketplace? The easy place is on the low end of the price scale. Beneath the highly-visible, upscale accounts is a huge array of lesser jobs, among them strip centers, smaller commercial buildings, and large numbers of older duplexes and residences.

You can earn a good living servicing these smaller accounts, without ever going big time at all.

> In older neighborhoods with small lots, mowing prices may be as low as $10 to $15 per job. But that doesn't mean you can't earn good money. The trick is to build **clusters** of jobs, so you have three or five or twelve lawns per stop. (How to do this is discussed in later chapters.) We had great success building clusters in our early years in business, in part because in older neighborhoods there is little competition worthy of the name.

While the downscale jobs I'm talking about can be located anywhere, they are especially prevalent in older, less-affluent parts of any city. Most northern cities have huge old blue-collar neighborhoods. Owners in these areas can't afford big outfits, which commonly have minimum prices of $50 or more per single stop. This huge portion of the market is left to little, low overhead outfits — in other words, to us.

Now, here's the thing to realize about entering this lower end of the market. At the moment, you have zero overhead expenses. No employees, no commercial building you must pay for — no nothing. That makes you an absolute killer competitor. If push comes to shove, you can make service stops clear down in the ten-buck range and still come out okay. Bigger outfits can't begin to do that. I suggest that you retain your low overhead advantage as long as you can.

Basically, that means running a home-based, solo operation. With minimal expenses, you can work profitably in the lower and middle portions of the market. Along the way you'll pick up fancy jobs too, but you can build a dandy bread-and-butter operation without a single one fancy job, without ever competing with the big dogs at all. You can always move up the scale later.

Equipment Purchases

What sort of equipment should you buy and when should you buy it? There's no sense going in hock right away. The safe, up-by-your-bootstraps approach is to start with as little as possible. If that means $50 worth of garage sale junk, so be it. That stuff won't last — it's not nearly tough enough for commercial work. But at least it will get you started and into a position where business income can be used to buy better machines.

When you reach that position — when cash flow will make the payments — then buy the biggest, fastest, most powerful commercial machine(s) that fit your jobs. Not the best you can afford, but the best available.

The reason to buy the best is that top notch equipment doesn't cost money, it earns money. Its speed and power allow it to pay for itself quickly, and keep right on earning.

For example, a long time ago I fractured our budget by buying a $4,500 commercial tractor. It paid for itself in five weeks. Eventually, we cut some $240,000 worth of grass with it!

True story: In the 1990s, a young guy named Art (not his real name) made quite a splash on the local mowing scene. New trucks, new trailers, gleaming new mowers, fancy airbrushed paint jobs on everything, even a nice piece of property and a stylish new building. It was Art, Art, Art everywhere you looked. He made some of us nervous. But not to worry, for his business soon bit the dust. Rumor has it that so did his father's lump sum retirement, $180,000. The moral of this sad story is that Art knew how to spend but not how to earn. Don't do that. Don't start at the top and hope it works. Start at the bottom. Learn how to earn good money in a small, low-risk operation. Then you can expand to your heart's content.

Today I see lots of kids trying to make money driving spiffy new bargain tractors from "big box" discount stores. They've made an awful choice. For one thing, using such a machine for commercial work voids the warranty. But that might not matter, for when (not if ... **when**) it blows up they won't be able to get it fixed anyway, because the discount store does not have a repair shop.

Even worse, bargain machines are too slow and inefficient to earn serious money. They limit income. It's as if you're saying, "I could earn $35 an hour this summer, but I don't want to. I want to earn $9 instead." Don't do that. Pinch pennies on everything else, but not on your main machines. Their speed and power will put money in your pocket, not take it out. See the equipment chapter for specific information on machines that fly and those that don't.

Two Business Models

As soon as you start dealing with customers, one of them is going to ask you if you clean gutters. Or trim shrubs. Or replace light switches. Or paint sheds or till gardens or trim trees or, I don't know, babysit kids. This, even though you offered only to mow the lawn. How wide a menu of services should you offer?

There are two views on the subject. You can offer 1) a narrow menu of services or 2) a broad menu of services. In the narrow view, you concentrate on one service: Mowing.

This narrow concentration allows you to buy the finest equipment on earth and to become extremely fast and efficient on the job. Efficiency translates to money. Working alone, I exceeded $50 per hour for years on end. Could I have done that as a jack of all trades? Not likely. The narrow menu also allows you to retain the home base/no paid help combination indefinitely. You remain the toughest price-competitor in town.

The broad view offers a different set of advantages. Many customers (both residential and commercial) would love to find a reliable "can-do" person to supply a wide range of services. If you don't supply these services, not only are you turning away money, you're also opening the door to competitors who will supply them. That's not the best idea. All things considered, a broad menu offers a better chance to build solid, long-term relationships with your customers.

But a broad menu has a downside, too. For one thing, it requires a lot of equipment, so you'll probably have to give up your home base/no-paid-help combo. That costs money. You won't be very efficient, either. You can't be perfect at everything, and that also costs money. To pay for all the people and things you need, your prices will have to go up. There goes your fierce competitive edge.

Even so, a broad menu is a step along the way to building a big outfit — the kind that holds the big, pricey contracts on major malls, condo complexes, and so on. At these top-of-the-heap levels, price competition is less important than the quality and scope of services offered. It's a different world.

For example, one fellow I read about, who sweeps mall parking lots for a living, bought a bucket truck to change outside lights at the malls. Does he make money doing this? No. But his customers like it, so the service gives him a major leg-up on his competitors. What to do when you're just getting started? I suggest that you offer a moderate range of services, renting equipment if necessary. See how it goes, see if you make money at it, see if you like it. Perhaps you will discover a tail that wags your mowing dog. Start with a moderate range and decide later whether to broaden your menu or narrow it.

Hint: When bidding commercial jobs such as strip centers and apartment complexes, you may frequently be asked to bid on lot sweeping, fertilizing, snow plowing, and similar jobs. Perhaps you won't be ready to do these jobs yourself for some time. But that doesn't mean you must turn them away. Consider subcontracting. We did this for years. Even today, my son has half-a-dozen subs lined up to help with the next blizzard. Needless to say, in this connection it pays to get to know your various competitors and develop friendly relations with them.

Sales Volume

In a small service business, sales volume — the total amount of money coming in — can be a highly misleading number. Come to think of it, it's a highly misleading number elsewhere too, as when a giant corporation grossing hundreds of millions of dollars a year suddenly goes belly-up. High sales volume didn't save them, and it won't save you, either. No matter how much money comes in, you can always spend more.

But people put stock in sales volume anyway. When new acquaintances find out you're self-employed, they always want to know how many employees and how many accounts you have, these being polite ways to find out if you amount to a pinch of ... snuff. Bigger, we all know, is better.

But people put stock in sales volume anyway. When new acquaintances find out you're self-employed, they always want to know how many employees and how many accounts you have, these being polite ways to find out if you amount to a pinch of ... snuff. Bigger, we all know, is better.

> For a part-time business, a reasonable first year goal is sales volume totaling $400 to $500 a week. A full-time operation might aim for $800 to $1,000. Modest as these amounts are, they can be made to yield decent profits, on the order of $350 and $700 respectively. But you won't make that much if you're a big spender. The trick is to hold business expenses, particularly labor, to the bare minimum.

If you admit to working alone, they smile and go talk to someone else. But is bigger really better? Does a business with ten employees earn more money than a one-person show? The answer is ... you don't know.

The bigger outfit could be slipping into bankruptcy. From the outside, there's just no way to tell.

Which brings me to the point: Don't chase sales volume.

Don't be fooled by people who brag about how many accounts and how many employees they have. They're just blowing smoke. Don't believe for one second that you're going to make more profit bringing in $4,000 per week than $1,000 per week. You might, and it stands to reason that you should. But there's nothing automatic about it.

Instead of pushing for high sales volume, I suggest that you aim for a moderate rate of growth. By adjusting your marketing efforts, you can make sales volume rise steadily, passing through $200 per week, $400 per week, $600, $800, and on up the line.

This gradual approach has two advantages. First, it gives you plenty of time to learn to handle heavy workloads without ripping your hair out. Second, it gives you time to develop an efficient — and therefore profitable — operation. As we'll see in later chapters, you can't buy efficiency in a store. It doesn't fall out of the sky, either. It's a thing you build, brick by thoughtful brick.

Worker Productivity

I've said that sales volume is not a good way to measure the health of your business. Odd as it may seem, neither is money in your pocket. You can be flush with cash and think you're on top of the world. But taxes and expenses are silently accruing, and machines are wearing out. You think you're doing great, and then one day you hit a brick wall. It happens all the time, and sometimes it's fatal.

Usually, small businesses avoid nasty surprises by hiring an accountant to do financial statements. But that's a bit much for a fledgling mowing business. Fortunately, there's an easier way, a single, simple, highly-reliable business yardstick that costs nothing and helps you manage your business every day. That yardstick is worker productivity.

> Though there are no firm rules, small mowing businesses commonly spend about one-third of gross income on expenses such as fuel, insurance, equipment, repairs, and so on. The remaining two-thirds (give or take) is divided between the employees and the owner. Just where you make the split is up to you. You can give your employees all of it, some of it, or — if you're as cheap as I am — none of it.

Worker productivity is expressed in dollars per man-hour. Suppose you have a job that pays $120. You spend four hours doing the work.

Here's how to calculate productivity:

$120 gross income ÷ 4 hours worked = $30 per man-hour.

Simple enough. But also enormously important.

Checking worker productivity is like putting your finger on the pulse of a heart patient. Instantly, you know what's going on inside, at the very center, where all is won or lost. In this case, at $30 per man-hour, the patient is doing fairly well. As long as you work alone from home, you can get by with low productivity numbers.

In a home-based solo operation, business expenses can be held so low that even a meager $10 to $15 per man-hour still nets more than a burger job. Such low numbers aren't desirable, but you aren't headed for welfare, either. It's when you start hiring help that productivity becomes critically important.

12

The rule of thumb is that each worker must produce twice her wages. I've never been comfortable with that figure; a minimum of three times wages is more to my liking.

Let's see how these numbers work in the example above, that $120 job.

Say you send two people out to do it, each earning $10 per hour. They're gone three hours, so you've used six hours of labor. That is, two people @ 3 hours each.

Then: $120 gross ÷ 6 hours worked = $20 per man-hour.

Since they are earning $10 per hour, your people are bringing in twice their wages, a borderline performance at best. Improvement is needed — faster machines, better crew training and supervision, higher prices for jobs.

Now perhaps you see why I recommend using the biggest, fastest, most powerful machines available. Their speed allows you to push productivity — and profits — right through the roof.

With small, slow machines, that simply is not possible. We'll discuss production numbers and their many uses in greater detail in a later chapter. I introduce the topic here only because some beginners think landing a job and sending out troops to do the work is quite enough. Maybe it is.

But don't bet on it. If your production numbers are low, your business is waving a huge red flag in your face. It's telling you you're earning little, or possibly nothing. The time to do something about it is now.

Customer Satisfaction

What's the most valuable asset your business has? That's easy: satisfied customers. Even if you have $40,000 worth of machinery, satisfied customers are still more valuable. Without them, you won't have any work for your machines to do. The lifeblood of a small service business is repeat business and referrals. Advertising is needed to get started, but after that you can enjoy years of steady growth without doing any advertising at all. Satisfied customers will grow your business for you.

We went from $900 per week to $2,400 per week without spending a penny on advertising. Over a longer period, a friend built his business from near nothing to $3,500 per week entirely through referrals. Most old pros have had similar, if less spectacular, experiences.

How do you put this magic to work for you? There are several do's and don'ts.

First, don't judge by appearances. Sooner or later, you're going to meet some scruffy dude who manages a rundown strip center, and later that day, a goofy old lady in a silly hat. It's easy to blow such people off, especially if you're really young or really dumb or, God forbid, both.

But consider this: His family might own 142 strip centers. She might be president of the Ladies Garden Club, with 1,200 wealthy members. Either of them could get you more high-paying jobs today than you can land on your own in a decade. No advertising or salesmanship needed ... these jobs are simply handed to you.

The first rule to getting word-of-mouth working for you is to can the kid stuff. **Be polite**. Treat everyone with respect, even deference. You never know who you're talking to.

Second, realize that while customers are not all the same, the overwhelming majority are happy if you do your work with ordinary competence. Your lawns should look better than most of the lawns in the neighborhood. Ordinary competence is a good job but not a perfect job. Good is what most people expect and are happy to get.

Third, most customers expect some measure of Three R's: Reasonable, Reliable, Responsible.

Reasonable refers to price, and means just what it says. Prices for services vary enormously, not only from city to city but within cities as well. For starters, your prices should be on the lower end of the scale. More on this later.

Reliable means ... well, reliable. If you tell a customer you'll be there at 4 PM Thursday, guess where you'll be at 4 PM Thursday? Lack of reliability is the Number One source of complaints about service businesses. Simply doing what you say you're going to do puts you a leg up on many of your competitors.

Responsible should read "responsible adult." I don't mean chronologically. Chronologically, nobody cares how old you are. What customers want is a person they can trust to treat their property as if it were their own. What customers absolutely despise is someone who comes to "work" equipped with a boom box, a cell phone, and two kibitzing buddies with jeans falling off their behinds.

It is essential to present the appearance and the reality of a workmanlike adult, even if you're only about six. If "responsible adult" is not your thing right now, flip burgers till it is.

To sum up, customers want you to be reasonable, reliable, and responsible, and they want work done competently.

To these four things you might add a kind of Boy Scout litany: polite, honest, cheerful, brave, clean, and reverent.

That's about it. Notice that nowhere on this list do you find charm, wit, charisma, etc. Customers aren't looking for personality, they're looking for performance. This is satisfactory to most customers, and a solid foundation on which to build your business.

Every now and then, though, you're going to run into a couple of other types of customers, namely cheapskates and perfectionists, for whom this act is just not good enough. The stock in trade of both types is talk. Talk, talk, talk. Always and ever, they want more. No matter what you do, it's never quite right, never quite enough. Always and ever, it's, "Let's make a deal."

Some contractors cater to these people, humoring them along, playing their endless games. Personally, I despise them. They're manipulators; they lay awake nights figuring out how to screw you. It's tempting to tell such people to put it where the sun doesn't shine.

But that can come back to bite you severely, in the form of negative referrals. It's safer to say "ram it" politely:

> "I'm making changes, Mrs. Smith, and won't be able to take care of your lawn any more. I'll cover it for now, but find someone else as soon as you can."

16

"Why, Mr. Adams," Mrs. Smith exclaims, "I thought everything was just peachy."

"You need to find someone as soon as you can, Mrs. Smith."

Competition

Finally we come to a topic that worries many beginners: All that competition out there.

How can you, little bitty you who knows nothing, possibly win?

Recently I read a story that provides the answer. It was about a man who saw a franchise business operation he really liked. He decided to buy one for himself. But that wasn't so easy. He had trouble contacting the home office. When he finally got through they put him off, saying they'd get back to him. They didn't.

After repeated tries, he finally made solid contact and arranged to visit the home office. But no one met him at the airport, no one arranged for transportation or a hotel. He had to do these things himself.

On and on the cold shoulder went; weeks of it. But finally the company softened up and started acting as it should. The man got his franchise and lived happily ever after.

Now, the point to this weird story is that the cold shoulder rigmarole was deliberate. The company was testing him. It had decided that it wanted tough-minded, determined people running its franchises. People willing to compete and win. The cold-shoulder routine was its way of weeding out the wimps.

Determination is a key ingredient in business success. The essential quality has many aspects and goes by many names, among them dedication, tough-mindedness, persistence, perseverance, self-reliance, resourcefulness, gumption, stick-to-itiveness, guts, intestinal fortitude, pluck, steadfastness, grit, backbone, tenacity, obstinacy, stubbornness, doggedness....

Whatever you call it, you're going to need it. When things go wrong — and sooner or later sixty-two things are going to go wrong on the same day — you can't go running to mama. There is no mama. You are being tested. What to do? Suck it up and go to work. If you don't know how to solve a problem, today is a good day to learn.

That sentence bears repeating:

If you don't know how to do something, today is a good day to learn.

Be aware that you aren't the only person going into business this month. Lots of people do it — there's always lots of competition. Perhaps you haven't noticed yet, but in the lawn business there's a major shakeout going on all the time.

Some beginners survive and prosper, but many more fall by the way.

Do you want to know who wins?

Here are some hints: It won't necessarily be the smartest gal, or the flashiest, or the richest. It won't necessarily be the guy with daddy's backing for all those fancy ads and fancy trucks and fancy uniforms, either. All that stuff is just window dressing.

You win by being tough. Like the man seeking the business franchise, you win by being unstoppable. Your job is to deliver a quality act to your customers, no matter what the circumstances. Your product is performance, not excuses.

Few beginning contractors understand these things and are willing or able to put together a rock-steady class act. When the going gets tough ... well, frankly, they blow it.

And when they blow it, their customers look for someone who flat refuses blow it. Someone they can count on. Someone unstoppable. That someone can be you.

This is how you create your own secure little fiefdom. Customers bounce around until they find a high quality service they can count on absolutely.

There they stay and stay and stay, and there they bring their friends.

All you have to do to win in the mowing business is deliver a class act consistently.

Then you'll never have to worry about your competitors.

They'll have to worry about you.

2. Preparations

Business start-ups are busy times. You'll have ads to run, calls to answer, estimates and jobs to take care of, bookkeeping to get used to ... a whole lot of busywork. Before taking the plunge, it's a good idea to get some of it out of the way. Some of the following items should be done, while others just need thinking about.

Small Business Administration

Want some free expert advice ... and maybe some cash to go with it? Check the federal government listings in the phone book and call the nearest Small Business Administration office. They can help with information and loans. You can also get free consultations with retired business executives through the CORE, the Corp of Retired Executives.

Form of Organization

Your business can be organized as a partnership or a corporation, both of which offer various subcategories. Perhaps there are advantages to one type or another ... talk to a lawyer or an accountant. In the meantime, if you do nothing, by default your business is a single or sole proprietorship. The chief implication of this is that you personally are liable for all debts of the business.

Fictitious Name

Are you going to be Fred's Lawn Service ... or The Greenskeeper? If you're going to use any name other than your own for the business, you'll have to register that name. Just who handles the matter varies from place to place. Get in the phone book and call county and state offices to find out.

Starter Rig

The ideal starter rig consists of a 36" commercial walk-behind mower, a trimmer, a blower, and an edger. (See Chapter 9 for details.) Everything rides on a trailer which is pulled by a pick-up truck.

Perhaps you'll have to start with less. That's fine — you have to do what you have to do. But smaller rigs are slow, whereas the recommended outfit is fast enough to earn serious money. So be prepared to move up quickly. Take time to visit equipment dealers in your area. Discuss price, delivery time, warranty, and financing. Most important, discuss repair service. Explain that you're going to mow commercially, and the machines you buy must be kept running.

Dealers who cater to commercial contractors ordinarily provide "next on the bench" privilege. That means that when you come in broken down, your repair is next, even though the shop may be weeks behind on homeowner repairs. If a dealer doesn't offer some such arrangement, find another dealer.

WARNING: NEVER BUY EQUIPMENT FROM A NON-SERVICING DEALER LIKE A HOME IMPROVEMENT WAREHOUSE.

Commercial use of cheap stuff exceeds design specifications by about twenty to one. Put another way, a machine designed to last a homeowner twenty years might last you twenty weeks. It's going to break, and when it does your warranty will almost certainly be void. Parts may be impossible to find and timely repair — any repair at all — not available. You don't need this kind of grief.

Base of Operations

Your base of operations consists of an office and a storage/maintenance facility for equipment. For starters, your office need be nothing more than a corner of the kitchen table or your computer.

> If you operate from home, you could qualify for a tax deduction called "business use of home." This means that a portion of certain household expenses — taxes, insurance, repairs — can be written off as "business expense." Savings can be substantial. However, rules governing this deduction are stringent, and claiming it is said to be a red flag to the IRS. Before you claim this expense, talk to a tax professional to be sure you qualify.

Operate from home if possible. If that's not possible, rent an inexpensive storage space big enough to hold a utility trailer with your equipment aboard. If you rent, check to be sure management allows equipment maintenance. Some do, some don't.

Eventually, you might want to rent a combined office/small warehouse space. These are ideal for service businesses, though rather expensive when you're just getting started. When setting up your storage/ maintenance facility, be aware that thieves often target turf equipment. Homeowners' insurance usually does not cover commercial-use equipment

Trade Area

When my son and I went into business, we hoped to create tight little routes within a few blocks of home. On about the second day, one of our neighborhood customers asked us to mow his apartment building, located in a suburb some eight miles away. A week later, we had three apartment buildings and two houses in that same suburb! So much for working right around home.

In a city of any size, due chiefly to contractor turnover, there are heaps of jobs up for grabs all the time. But they aren't necessarily in the upscale subdivisions you've chosen as favored turf. They might be anywhere, including on the wrong side of the tracks.

Plan to cast a wide advertising net. Go where the jobs are. If you don't already know it, you'll soon learn that there are profitable jobs and helpful, friendly people everywhere. If you must weed out your routes, do it later when you have too many jobs, not now, when you have too few.

Commercial vs. Residential

Recently I heard from a beginner who planned to mow only commercial jobs, such as businesses and offices. Just how he planned to do this — and why — was never made clear. But I told him I thought it was a mistake.

The chief advantage to commercial jobs is that money arrives in big chunks. For years, our top single job was a seventeen-acre apartment complex that paid $435 per mowing (first year price.) Three of us (two on tractors and one trimming and blowing) would knock that beast out by ten o'clock Monday morning. That's a dandy way to start your work week.

If money in big chunks is the advantage to larger commercial jobs, the drawback is that every ambitious contractor in town knows about them, and wants them, and bids on them. Competition can be fierce. Contracts ordinarily last only a year, and then you have to start your business over. It can be a jungle.

Few residential jobs pay $435 per week or anything remotely like it. On the other hand, they are far easier to get, and you can often keep them indefinitely without competitive bidding. Life here, it turns out, is fairly smooth. Plus which, though it might take a while, you can build large clusters of residential lawns that pay very well indeed.

For example, one local outfit that has been in business twenty-some years has a "stop" where the trucks trundle slowly up one street and down the next, while crews mow small residential lawns for hours on end without shutting off the machines. I'd guess that one stop is worth $1,000 or more. I'll discuss building clusters of jobs later.

What types of jobs are best? Personal preference — doing what you like to do — definitely counts.

For my money, the best jobs are commercial properties (apartments, businesses, offices) that are locally-owned and managed. Big national chains are okay, but not ideal. Onsite managers are liable to change without warning, corporate edicts come floating down from on high, and so on. To big outfits, we little folk are readily expendable. You stand a better chance of building a good, lasting relationship with local management/owners.

When you're getting started, don't make any hard rules regarding residential versus commercial jobs. The same advertising and sales techniques will acquire both, and references are a two-way street, with residential customers wanting you to take care of their businesses and vice versa. For now, just let your business go where it wants to go. You can decide whether or not to specialize later, when you've gained more experience.

Communications

How are you going to communicate with your customers? Years ago, not wanting baby sister to answer "Goo-goo!" when Mr. Big Shot called, we used various options, including private phone lines into the house, recorders, and professional answering services. These days, the hands-down winner is a cell phone and voice mail. Get in the habit of answering your phone in a professional manner by stating your name or your company name.

Also set up a dedicated email account, for your business only. Check it every day, and respond to your customers promptly and professionally.

Insurance Coverages

You'll need several types of insurance. First, you'll need liability for property damage or personal injury resulting from business operations. This covers accidents on the job.

Second, you may need commercial insurance for your vehicle. Then again, maybe not. Check with your insurance agent to be sure.

Third, if you plan to hire anyone, you'll need workers' compensation insurance. This covers you if someone is hurt on the job. The name of this coverage varies from state to state, as does the carrier; some states carry it themselves while others use private carriers. Check with your insurance agent for details.

Permits

Will you need a vendor's license? Will you have to collect and pay sales tax?

Requirements vary from city to city and state to state. If you happen to know a bookkeeper or an accountant, that's the person to ask. If not, get in the phone book and call local and state offices in your area to find out what's required. In my experience, local governments favor the formation of new business, so requirements are usually quick and painless.

Backup Positions

Suppose you're on the job for three months, and everything is going great, and one day a bus runs over your foot. Now what? Do you lose your business because of an accident?

Later on, when your business has grown to the level of several employees, back-up may not be a problem. Employees worth having can handle things temporarily, with little or no supervision.

But early on, when you're working alone, it's a good idea to have someone who can fill in.

Perhaps this is a partner, spouse, family member, friend, or even a friendly competitor. Once, when I was kidnapped and forced to go fishing in Canada for a week, a friendly rival took care of my accounts for me. No problems.

Machines also need backing up, but that's easy. Failing quick repairs or loaner machines from your dealer, your backup is cash or credit. Just buy what you need.

Personal Finances

Some business start-up guides recommend that before going into business you set aside enough money to live on for a year. Hah! If we really had to do that, you'd see precious few new businesses out there.

Even so, personal finances need consideration. Realize, for example, that except as you provide them yourself, you'll have no benefits: no medical insurance, no unemployment insurance, no workers' compensation, no paid vacations, holidays, or retirement.

Realize, too, that it's not a good idea to count on income from the business. You could get off to a slow start. But even if you start fast, early income should be left in the business to build up a reserve. A reserve is needed, for taxes and other expenses are silently accruing and will have to be paid eventually. Also, you'll want to obtain top-of- the-line equipment as soon as you can.

To handle your money properly, open a checking account to be used for business only. No personal transactions here. Deposit all money that comes into the business into the account. Pay all business expenses out of the account. Pay yourself out of the account, too, by writing yourself a paycheck for the same set amount each week.

Leave all other money in the account as a reserve, at least until you have built up a hefty balance.

Shifting Gears

Suppose you've decided to keep your day job and mow lawns part-time, roughly twenty hours a week. You line up equipment and start running ads in local papers.

What's going to happen? No one knows. But normally, nothing spectacular happens. You start getting calls, start doing estimates, start mowing lawns. Usually, things are fairly peaceful. It takes a while to build a client list.

Usually, but not always. You might be hoping for $600 per week and suddenly find yourself with $1,600. How? Well, you might bid a single strip mall, and the next day the owner calls and wants you to do all twenty-two of his properties. Or you might wander in where some other outfit just went out. That happened to us once, and in hours we had a single stop with twenty-some fancy little lawns totaling over $600 per week. Flyer distributions (discussed later) can also produce startling results.

What to do? First, expect this sort of thing to happen. Not right away, perhaps, but if you hang around this business any length of time, sudden leaps in the workload become highly likely.

Second, when it happens, do not hire the first warm bodies you see and send them out to do the work while you go about business as usual. They might do the work. Then again, they might spend the day in the park, checking out girls. You must stay close all the time. Otherwise, you won't have to worry about all those new jobs for long. Somebody else will be worrying about them.

Third, understand that mowing hours are highly flexible. There's no such critter as a "40-hour mowing route." Double the number of people and machines, and your "40-hour route" takes maybe 23 hours. Double again and you're down to perhaps 13 hours. (Due to inefficiencies with larger crews, doubling up never quite cuts time in half.)

All this is as simple as it sounds (well ... make that almost as simple.) By adding or subtracting people and machines, you can handle enormously varied workloads without changing your own hours significantly. That's what experienced contractors do all the time. It should not be otherwise when you're just getting started.

But you can't shift gears smoothly if you're not prepared. So do your homework now. Know exactly who you are going to hire: family, friends, relatives, perhaps help from a temporary agency such as Manpower. Also do your shopping now. Know exactly which machines you're going to buy and where you're going to buy them. Know the price, delivery time, warranty, financing. In short, be ready. All it costs is a little time.

Billing and Bookkeeping

A full-scale discussion of business bookkeeping is beyond the scope of this guide. However, you are going to need some sort of bookkeeping system, and the time to get it in place is now, before you begin operations.

> Sometimes, a reader asks me if there is some kind of "student" business category, so they can avoid bookkeeping, taxes, and leaps through assorted bureaucratic hoops. They're asking the wrong person; I'm not a tax pro. As far as I know, though, there is no such deal. The only way I know of to avoid paying taxes is to be really, really rich.

There are three basic choices. One is the old-fashioned way, where you use such antiques as pencils and paper. I kept books this way for twenty-some years. A little knowledge is needed, but that's easy to come by in the public library. Handy forms for this method are available at office supply stores.

A second method is to use a computer program designed for your specific type of business. My son uses an inexpensive program called Gopher to handle scheduling, bidding, and billing, and farms out the rest. A quick

Google search for "bookkeeping software" got some four million hits, among them Gopher, QuickBooks and Lawn Pro ... so the topic seems to be covered. Bookkeeping software is definitely the way to go in the future, but the money might better be spent on something else when you're just getting started.

A third choice is to hire a business bookkeeping firm. They can set you up with an easy do-most-of-it-yourself system and provide such help with payroll and tax accounting as you need. Costs are reasonable.

Finally, let me make a suggestion on an extremely important topic: Payroll accounting. It's not unusual for beginning contractors to hire friends or family members and pay them "under the table" or pretend that they're "independent contractors" so payroll taxes and workers' comp are avoided. **This is a huge mistake**.

All sorts of troubles loom, among them the possibility of a serious accident. You could get a judgment against you that follows you into old age.

Do yourself a big favor: Do it right.

3. Advertising

The purpose of advertising is to make contact with potential customers. When someone responds to your ad, you make an appointment to inspect the proposed job and bid, or give a price estimate.

For residential contacts, you can reasonably expect to sell about half the jobs you estimate. For commercial contacts, competition is stiffer, so your conversion rate will probably be lower. But your conversion rate — and, for that matter, the pulling power of your ads — is not terribly important. Repeat business and referrals are the lifeblood of a mowing business. Even if the influx of new customers from advertising is rather feeble, your business still ought to grow like a snowball rolling downhill. Slowly, maybe, but rolling. If it doesn't, you probably need to improve in the area of customer satisfaction. Advertising, then, has a limited purpose.

Advertising Methods

Here are eleven advertising methods, along with my impression of their effectiveness.

Acquaintances: You might not think that the construction worker-dude eating breakfast a few stools down the counter is looking for a lawn service. Maybe he isn't. But his grandmother could be. Which is to say, let people know what you are doing. Work, school, church, bowling alley, shopping mall, park, the insurance office, the doctor's office ... wherever you rub elbows, mention what you are doing. Don't ignore this method and don't underestimate it. Casual acquaintances can be a very significant source of jobs, and they don't cost a cent.

Shoppers' Papers: These are the little local newspapers that are practically all advertising. Often they're distributed weekly, often for free. Classified ads are really cheap, typically starting at a couple of bucks. That's the problem. Every neighborhood kid with two bucks runs an ad. Response is usually weak. Even so, because ads cost little, any response at all is a bargain. On balance, it's worth placing small classifieds in these papers, but don't count on them to build a business anytime soon.

Metropolitan Dailies: Ads placed in big daily newspapers are expensive. But the cost keeps the kids out and circulation is enormous, so ads placed here draw a powerful response. You'll have to check your own results, of course, but usually the big dailies are well-worth the cost.

Notices: A notice is a flyer posted on a bulletin board in a laundromat, bowling alley, or other neighborhood location. The response to notices is limited. But this is another freebie that's definitely worth doing.

Truck Signs: Not tested, but said to produce a strong response.

Business Cards: Definitely worth having, particularly for introducing yourself.

Chamber of Commerce: Not tested, but included because I know a South Florida man who built a nice little property maintenance business solely by registering with the Chamber of Commerce. He lived in a fast-growing area.

Yellow Pages: Could be valuable down the road, but expensive and therefore questionable when you're just getting started.

> You'll get the most bang for your advertising buck during a five- or six-week period centered on the start of the mowing season. In Toledo, the starting date is about April 15th; check with local mower dealers for the date in your area. Ads run at other times might still draw a respectable response, though it's advisable to test cautiously before spending much money. Also, try timely offers, such as spring "yard clean-up" or fall "leaf clean-up" specials.

Internet: When we built our business, little of the present Internet existed, so I lack personal experience using this method. But times have changed. These days, lots of small mowing outfits have web sites, advertise on Craigslist, and (perhaps) use social media. Advertising by these means is so cheap that any response at all is a bargain, so there's no reason not to do it. I have only one suggestion: If you choose to build a website, make it a commercial site, so it will be picked up by the search engines. The personal sites provided free by ISPs are ignored in web searches.

Flyers: Flyers are expensive, especially if you pay for professional distribution. But they offer three advantages over other advertising means.

1. **Length of the advertising message**. An old rule of advertising says, "The more you tell,

the more you sell." With a flyer you have an entire page to sell your service.

2. **Pinpoint distribution.** Other advertising methods tend to draw responses from all over creation, which can mean a lot of driving between jobs. With flyers, you can target a single street, neighborhood, or subdivision.

3. **Longevity.** I once got a phone call from a lady who'd kept my flyer for seven years!

In my experience, flyers draw phone calls with a vengeance. But to build business, you must distribute at least several thousand, and that's expensive. Flyers are excellent for well-defined targets, though, such as breaking into a new neighborhood or filling in around existing jobs.

Occasionally, a reader asks me how much it costs to acquire a customer by advertising. The answer is ... I haven't the faintest idea. But I'd say dollar-for-dollar is a good return; that is, one $20 ad landing one $20 job. In our second season we spent $700 on flyers and landed $900 a week in new business in a matter of days — a huge bargain. (See the Appendix.) All things considered, though, advertising cost means little. In the mowing business a customer might stay with you twenty years, spent thousands of dollars, and bring scores of new customers via word of mouth. So whether you spent $10 or $50 acquiring him doesn't mean a whole lot.

Bribery: That guy down the block with the fertilizer trucks gets asked about mowing services every day. People who clean carpets get asked about handyman services. Handymen get asked about cleaning services. And so on. Get to know your fellow service people. Offer to swap or buy referrals. Am I kidding? Absolutely not.

Bribery is an excellent source of jobs. I once bribed a fertilizer guy for two jobs in a fancy subdivision that turned out to be lawyer heaven. Everybody knew everybody, and within a year that stop grew to twenty-two jobs worth over $500.

Cold Calling

Most residential jobs are obtained through the advertising methods mentioned above or by referral. You'll also pick up some commercial accounts this way. But the vast majority of commercial contracts are awarded through competitive bids. These people won't come looking for you, so you must call upon them.

A mowing friend of mine uses a cold-calling technique to contact potential customers in upscale residential areas, where he has developed highly-profitable clusters of jobs. He looks up targeted properties in the county real estate office. This gives him a good deal of information. He then contacts the owner, makes an appointment, and submits his bid.

The first step is to decide which jobs you want. You can aim at any target in sight, but if you're just getting started, bear in mind that huge, upscale contracts are likely to be very demanding. You'll need experience to handle them. Polish your act on little fish before going for big fish.

Once you've set targets, spy on them. See which services are being performed at the property and who is doing them, how often, what time of day, and how long it takes. Start developing your own competing bid.

At the same time, find out who is in charge of grounds maintenance contracts. This is easier than it sounds, for someone who is onsite much of the time knows who that person is. Perhaps it's the owner or the store manager. With strip centers, the manager of any of the stores knows who manages the property. In the case of chains — fast food, auto parts, drugs, groceries, and so on — it's probably some regional bigwig or a large property management firm, perhaps out-of-state.

In any case, ask until you find out who to deal with. Then, when you're ready, make an appointment with the appropriate local manager to submit your bid. When dealing with out-of-state firms, communication is via the Internet, phone, email, and fax.

When considering commercial jobs, don't overlook subsidized apartment complexes. Midwestern cities contain lots of them, often scattered all over town. In my experience, the larger complexes have onsite offices and full-time managers. The manager is your initial contact. Probably you will be referred to the office of a local property management firm that works for the investors and manages not just the one complex, but five ... or fifteen. This can be an opening to serious money indeed. We found this work highly lucrative.

Advertising Copy

Writing short classified ads to promote your business is no particular challenge. Local newspapers are filled with free examples placed by your competitors. While you never know for sure, it's reasonable to assume that an ad that runs week after week, long-term, is drawing a satisfactory response. Emulate these successful ads, adding your own personal touch, and you should draw an adequate response.

Besides short ads, you'll also need a long ad, roughly a full page. This long ad is the basis for display ads, flyers, notices, and a hand-out sheet or brochure to be given to prospects when making sales calls. (See the next chapter.) It will also help you to clarify and articulate your message when promoting your business.

As with short ads, you might want to model your long ad after an existing successful ad. How do you know an ad is successful? If it runs repeatedly in expensive media — television, national magazines, large daily newspapers — you can be fairly certain it is working. No one repeats failing ads in these expensive media because no one can afford to.

Less reliable media include the Internet and the endless stream of home improvement flyers that attach themselves to my front door (kind of gives you the idea that your house needs improving.) Many of these flyers are blatantly amateurish, and should be ignored. As to Internet advertising, space is so cheap that almost anyone could run a failed ad indefinitely.

You'll want to emulate successful ads. Also, you'll want to structure ads logically, so that one idea flows naturally from another. Though there are endless variations, a great many successful ads follow this basic formula:

This formula has been used to sell everything imaginable for at least 150 years. It has become so familiar that we tend to look right at it without seeing it. Plugging your own advertising message into this proven formula is no great challenge. If that's the route you choose, here a few things to keep in mind.

Sequence and Content: The formula presents your advertising message in a natural sequence, showing the reader the many ways he will benefit from your service, offering a special bargain for signing up now, and showing him how to do it.

Features versus Benefits: Advertising gurus tell us to sell benefits, not features — the sizzle, not the steak. What does that mean?

A **feature** is an attribute of something: "This car has four headlights."

A **benefit** is what that feature does for you: "With four headlights you can see a safe distance ahead at night."

Here are a four features and a benefit each of them provides.

Feature: "Mow your lawn."

Benefit: "Let us keep your lawn looking extra-sharp this season."

Feature: "Paint your house."

Benefit: "Give your home a fresh new look."

Feature: "Reasonable prices."

Benefit: "Save $25 today!"

Feature: "Cooking timer."

Benefit: "Set it and forget it!"

Headline
(Promises the reader a strong benefit)

Subheading
(Clarifies headline; promises additional benefit)

Benefit
Benefit
Benefit
Benefit

Credentials
Our tenth year! Billions served.

Action step
(Puts a premium on acting now.)
Call today to get this special price.)

Contact information

(The last example shows up on late-night TV all the time. It's Ron — "But wait! There's more!" — Popeil, of course. He is one of the great pitchmen of our age. His book *The Salesman of the Century* is a fun read.)

There's no mystery to features and benefits. You simply take a feature and express it in human terms, thus turning it into a benefit. That's what you must do when writing flyers. The first draft or two might promise all sorts of features, but in later drafts express them as benefits. Benefits draw a stronger response.

Note, note, NOTE: You must to enumerate benefits to the reader. It's fine if you are a former crack addict who is mowing lawns to save for a new wooden leg for your grandmother. Very nice and ... who cares? As a potential customer, I want to know what your service will do for me, not for you.

Action Step: The purpose of the action step is overcome the reader's tendency to procrastinate. We read an offer and say to ourselves, "I think I'll do this," or "This sounds pretty good." But then we tend to set it aside and forget about it.

Special, This Week Only, and *Call Today to Get These Special Prices* are typical action steps. You can see and hear scores more in TV ads for cheapo mail order products, as in a current spot in which they offer one broom for $29.95. (It's a hell of a broom, or at least a hell of a pitch for a broom.) But wait. They immediately back down to one broom for $10. In seconds, it's two brooms for $10. But only, of course, if you call immediately.

That's a classic action step. Advertisers include actions steps because they work.

Professionalism: Be aware that a flyer or other long ad may be the only part of your business a prospect sees. To her the flyer is your business. Now, you may be an absolute master at manicuring lawns to perfection. But a flyer with poor production values — misspellings, grammatical errors, and so on — tells the prospect you are sloppy. Maybe you aren't, but that's what it says. And that won't do at all.

Fortunately, any word processor you're likely to encounter these days will help immeasurably in producing error-free work. Or you can have someone knowledgeable — a teacher, say, or a secretary — proofread your flyer for you.

Finally, many of the amateurish flyers I see show signs of being dashed off on the way up my driveway. Do not waste your money distributing such stuff.

Start working on your flyer early, at least several weeks before you intend to use it. Write a first draft and set it aside for a few days. Come back with fresh eyes — you'll be amazed at how much more you can see. Do this several times. Don't be in a hurry to get into print. Instead, let your work evolve, getting better with age. Good ads pay big dividends. For a copy of a flyer that pulled with a vengeance, see the Appendix.

Words that Sell

Here are some terms that are highly effective in flyers:

Free	Bargain	Best	Complete
Exclusive	Fun	First	How to
New	Save Money	Profitable	Powerful
Easy	Fast	Afford	Special
Affordable	Limited Offer	Better	Sale
Guaranteed	Special Offer	Save	Secret
Improved	Make Money	Call Today	Act Now

4. Selling

Selling property maintenance services is probably the easiest selling job in the world. When you think about it, most prospects actively seek you — they called you up, didn't they? And you're seeking them. So you've got desire on both sides. That being the case, turning contacts into customers often amounts to nothing more than working out the details — price, specific service, frequency, and so on. Further to the same point, when closing the sale, you don't need a death-do-us-part commitment. People can try your service for a week or two while risking virtually nothing. It all adds up to very easy selling.

The only hitch in the process is the fact your competitors are trying to sign up the same customers. Most of the prospects who answer your ads also call other contractors, to get a sense of the market — what's being offered, for how much money, and so on.

Who gets the sale? Price is always a factor. I've never been in a negotiation where the cheapest bidder did not have a shot. I hate to keep harping on the same point, but this is why it's important to keep overhead expenses down, so you can bid low.

But price isn't the only factor. Remember, the prospect called you because she has a problem. She's looking for the best person to solve that problem. Cheap, yes. But also skilled and honest and reliable — someone she can count on not only today but in the future.

It's your job to be that trustworthy person.

Estimating Prices

An estimate, or bid, is a price quote. "I'll mow your lawn for $40."

Accurate estimates are important. If you bid jobs too high, you won't get many, and those you do get may soon be lost to lower bidders.

On the other hand, if you bid too low you could wind up working hard for little money. So it's important to get it right.

What is the correct price for a job? The correct price is a number that is satisfactory to both you and your customer for at least one season. You are making reasonable money, and the customer perceives that she is not being ripped off. That's the correct price.

Please don't write to me asking for a universal scale of correct prices, or a nationwide scale, or a citywide scale, or even a block-wide scale. Except as you set it yourself, there is no scale. This deal is between you and your customer, one on one.

To determine the area of a property (in square feet):

Rectangular: Width (feet) x Depth (feet) = Area (sq. feet)

Triangular (or pie-slice): Width x Depth ÷ 2 = Area

Trapezoidal: Front Width + Rear Width x Depth ÷ 2 = Area

How do you begin? Start by setting a minimum price per stop. I don't know where you live and can't tell you what your minimum should be, but it's hard to see how you can make out mowing lawns these days for less than $10 to $15 each. This applies even to tiny lots in rundown neighborhoods. If an area won't pay even that little bit, advertise somewhere else.

The minimum price is for tiny lawns. But most lawns today are large enough to pay far more than your minimum price. You can set your scale for these lawns in either of two ways. One method is based on time. Mow your own lawn, along with those belonging to friends, neighbors, and relatives. Keep time and then work out a price for each job, based on a gross rate of perhaps $15 to $25 per hour.

Thus do you establish a scale: lawns this size are $12, lawns that size $28, and so on.

> When measuring residential properties, use lot lines only, with no deduction for house or driveway, etc. When measuring commercial properties such as strip centers, which are mostly pavement and buildings, measure only the actual area to be mowed.

You can also set a scale based on area. Begin by setting a rate — for starters, perhaps $1 to $1.50 — per thousand square feet. Then determine the area of the property you're estimating, multiply by your rate, and that's your price.

For example, suppose you pace off the front and side lot lines of a property (or measure them with a wheel) and determine that it is 200 feet by 200 feet.

The lot measures 40,000 square feet.

Multiply 40,000 by $1 per thousand and you get $40.

Multiply 40,000 by $1.50 and you get $60.

Your price range for this lawn is $40 to $60.

Can you mow 40,000 square feet — the better part of an acre — for $40 to $60?

It depends on how you do it. With the high-efficiency operation I ran for years — big fast tractor, no wasted motion, no slowpokes to nursemaid (see Chapter 8) — this price range is excellent. I mowed many such lawns and loved every minute of it.

On the other hand, a slow, sloppy, outfit bogged down with foot-dragging troops would probably find $40 to $60 impossibly unprofitable. Whatever the case, this raw price gives you a place to start. Usually it's not the final price. In nearly all cases it will have to be adjusted.

As your business matures, you'll probably have jobs you no longer want — distant, difficult, poor-paying. So too with equipment. The stuff you started with is probably slow and weary. What to do? Surprise, surprise! Worn-out equipment plus bad customers equals a lawn mowing business to sell! Try not to buy one of these turkeys.

Because of the need for adjustments, you cannot estimate jobs sight-unseen. Only when you're on the ground looking at the property can you see what you're getting into.

Here are some things to consider:

Location, location, location. Is the job two minutes from your main route ... or two hours away?

Is the job in an area where you plan to (and probably can) build up your business in the future ... or do you see no good reason to drive clear over there?

Is the property in Big Bucks Acres or Dog Patch? Try to charge big bucks in Dog Patch and you won't land a whole lot of jobs.

Does the property have a narrow gate which will require a tiny, slow mower in that huge backyard? Someone has to pay for all that extra time.

Standard operating procedure in most parts of the country is to give customers a weekly mowing price, then bill them once a month through the season. Florida is different. SOP there is to bill customers a uniform monthly rate year round. This covers four or five mowings per month during the growing season and fewer mowings, perhaps only one or two per month, in winter. For local details, check with your mower dealer.

Are you going to bag the grass clippings (slow and expensive) ... or let them fly (quick and cheap)?

Is the property a flat, dusty, wide-open weed patch you can "tractor" in ten minutes ... or is it luxurious, plastic-flamingo-infested maze that will have to be manicured for three solid hours every week, assuming you don't get lost?

Your own efficiency is a major factor in pricing. Efficiency has everything to do with the prices you charge. Run a really tight ship, and you can mow cheaper than the other guy and earn more money doing it.

Personal preferences also enter into the equation. Are you a gardener-sort, content to peck away at careful detail work? Or would you rather light up a fast tractor and fly? There are plenty of jobs of both kinds. It turns out, then, that lot size is not the only factor in determining mowing price. Often it is not even the most important. The points noted above mean every bit as much.

Finally, we get to the bottom line. What you are really looking for when setting prices is time and effort. You do not have an unlimited supply of either. So you want know how much impact this job will have, how much it will take out of you. You want to know how big a dent it will make in your work week.

If a lawn is close, quick, and easy, you can do it cheap. If it's distant, difficult and demanding, you must make it expensive.

These variables mean that mowing prices vary not just a little, but by huge margins. Let me give you an example. Years ago in a fancy golf course development, we and other outfits mowed one-acre luxury home sites for $75 to $95 each. These were tough jobs, highly demanding. At the same time, working alone on a big fast tractor, I flew around a plumbing contractor's dandelion patch for about the same money, $85. But it wasn't one acre, it was five. If my math is correct, we're talking a five hundred percent size variation here. But that's how estimating works, or should work: Easy is easy and tough is tough.

This lopsided price arrangement — $15 per easy acre, $75 per tough acre — continued for years, with all concerned happy as clams. It occurs to me that this section on estimating is getting awfully long and, perhaps, confusing. If so, don't worry about it.

Just do your estimates and go to work. Especially at first, you're going to be a little off — too high here, too low there. But you're always a little off, no matter how long you are in business. It's not a thing to lose sleep over. Just do your best and learn from your mistakes.

Finally, if you hang around this business a while, you'll start seeing the world as experienced mowing contractors see it — in terms of neighborhoods, subdivisions, and dollar signs.

Tell me what neighborhood phone call came from in the western half of Toledo, and I automatically visualize typical houses and lots in the area, along with mowing prices.

For example, I know that there is very little in the huge west end neighborhood where I grew up that's over $15. On our scale, the palaces in the Brandywine subdivision were $75 and up, Ragan Woods $25 to $35, smaller lots in Corey Woods about the same, Lincoln Woods a bit less.

And so on and on.

To avoid nasty surprises, we always looked at a property before committing to a price, but that was, years ago, our scale. You'll establish your own scale quickly enough.

The Salesperson

What should you drive when you go out selling? What should you wear?

Appearance is important. Prospects have little enough to judge you on, so fair or not, they're going to form an impression based on what they see. Wheel up in your Beamer wearing a loud sport coat and you'll make one impression. Rumble up on a Harley wearing your *Shit Happens* t-shirt and you'll make quite another. Fortunately, it's easy to make the proper visual impression.

Start with good grooming. *Always* start with good grooming.

As to transportation, your work vehicle is fine if it's in presentable condition. If you can see through the fenders, though, it's a good idea to borrow something better for calls in upscale residential and commercial areas.

As to clothing, strike a happy medium by wearing what you expect the prospect to wear. Working people in ordinary neighborhoods wear clean work clothes and will expect the same of you. For meeting with the Building and Grounds Maintenance Supervisor for GM Midwest, upgrade to your Sunday-go-to-meetin' duds. As to the latest teen style, your friends are the best judges. If they love it, for God's sake don't wear it.

As to attitude, quiet confidence, positive thinking, a positive mental attitude — these are attributes mentioned in every book on sales. I lump them together under *enthusiasm*.

Enthusiasm means that you enjoy what you do, and are convinced that it's the right thing for your prospect as well. You're sharing good news and you're excited about it. Your excitement is infectious. The prospect catches it and buys.

Sales gurus agree than enthusiasm is extremely important; many think it's the most powerful sales tool of all. Where does enthusiasm come from?

Rah-rah sales meetings are one common source. Another source is rituals, as found in books on selling. These take the form of poems, prayers, and catchy sayings that you mouth repeatedly, psyching yourself up. If these kinds of gimmicks work for you, be my guest. But frankly they seem unnecessary.

You have a powerful source of enthusiasm that is entirely natural — not one speck of phoniness about it. That source is your business itself. Are you El Sloppo Painting Service? Quick and Dirty Lawn Care? Rip Off Black Top?

I hope not. I hope you are determined to be an honest and straightforward business person who gives your customers first-rate service at fair prices. Prospects call you because they have problems. Make it your business to provide first-rate solutions to those problems. Once you've decided to you give every customer a fair, honest deal, then you have every reason to be enthusiastic.

For the fact is, customers don't always get good deals. Those of middle age or older have almost certainly been abused by assorted incompetents and ripoff artists. If you don't believe me, ask them. They'll tell you tales of woe that'll make you laugh and cry at the same time. Make it your business to be the good, honest service provider the prospect has been looking for all these years. If that's not something to be positive and enthusiastic about, I don't know what is.

You'll be far ahead in the sales game if you make it a rule always to treat prospects as potential friends. If you do, many will become actual friends, at least on a casual basis. They'll help you and in countless ways, not least in the form of referrals.

Finally, be aware that top salespeople don't overwhelm prospects with chat or information. Instead, they ask questions and listen carefully to the answers. People will tell you lots of things, including what they want to buy and how to close the deal, if only you will listen.

The Presentation

You have an appointment. Arrive neither late nor early but on time. Before meeting the prospect, give the property a quick once-over. Is it neat, clean, well-manicured? Just average? Or is it rundown and sloppy? These are important clues to customer expectations. It's easy to sell 'em when you know what they want.

When meeting a prospect, always introduce yourself and your company ("Hello. I'm Jim Adams of Adams Mowing. Are you Mrs. Smith?") Offer a handshake and a smile, and hand them something — either a business card or a flyer or brochure describing your services. Until they tell you otherwise, all prospects have one of two names: Mr. or Mrs.

After a brief bit of get acquainted chit-chat, it's time to demonstrate your product. That's easy enough if you're selling vacuum cleaners. But how do you demonstrate mowing?

You might use photos of fancy lawns you maintain. You might drop names of clients in the neighborhood. But your best bet for clear communication is the brochure you just handed the prospect.

Be aware that people call you for reasons of their own. Maybe they want you to mow only until they get their machine out of the shop. Maybe they want you to serve as backup when Cousin Willie has the DTs. Maybe ... well, maybe all sorts of waste-your-time crapola.

Find out what they want. Go through your brochure (or a checklist) point by point.

"Are you interested in regular weekly mowing, ma'am?"

"Fertilizing?"

"When the time comes, would you be interested in having us trim those shrubs over there?"

Sometimes this Q&A yields surprising insights into a prospect's mindset. Once, I asked a seemingly sweet little old lady if she wanted her sidewalks edged.

"Edging?" she said. "I don't care about edging. Just mow the son of a bitch."

Whatever the case, find out what the prospect wants. Then you can package up a deal for her: "We can do this, this, and this, and this is how much it will cost."

Your typical vacuum cleaner salesman doesn't have this flexibility. He's got his Nimbus 2000 and that's pretty much it. You have the enormous advantage of making up a custom product that fits the prospect's needs on the spot.

Will she buy your product instantly? Maybe. Often as not, though, people want to ho-hum a bit. Most of us are like that: we don't like to make an earth-shattering (or not) decision today if we can put it off till tomorrow. So it's not unusual for a prospect to want to "think it over," or "talk it over with my husband," etc. These are delaying tactics. Meeting them with a heavy-handed close is a mistake.

She wants certain jobs done and you want to do them. So it's simply a matter of working out the details. The working-out process is a soft negotiation, a bit of low-key dickering between people on their way to becoming friends. Behind her delaying tactic might be real objections. She wants the work done, yes, but she also wants to be sure she's choosing the right person to do it.

Your salesperson's touchstone here is the Three R's: Reasonable, Reliable, and Responsible. As opportunities in the conversation allow, stress that you do your best to hold prices down; that you are absolutely reliable; and that you treat a customer's property as if it were your own.

Another area of possible objections involves your work experience (or the lack of it.) Don't stretch it. Tell the truth. If you've done lots of these types of jobs, say so: "No problem, Mrs. Smith. We do these all the time." If you lack experience ... well, the new guy on the block always tries harder, doesn't he? Often, prospects are looking for someone who can do a whole lot more than just the minimum. She called you because she has an immediate problem, yes. But that might only be the beginning.

The fact is, many people these days are very, very busy. Single-parent and two-earner families are commonplace, as are business and professional people who put in sixty to eighty hours per week. Managers of stores and other enterprises also live hectic schedules, with dozens of irons in the fire all the time. They are looking for someone to unburden them. You can be that person.

Let them know that they can take this whole nagging bag of busywork and dump it on you. "You don't have to worry about any of that stuff that any more, Mrs. Smith. I'll take care of it."

Unburdening is especially important to senior citizens. We've worked long and hard for our freedom (and don't we just love to rub it in to you spring chickens), and we don't give it up easily. We want to go visit the grandkids at the drop of a hat, without having to worry about the damned lawn. We worried about it for forty years. Enough, already.

Now it's your turn to worry about it. So important is this unburdening that I used to think of my service as a public utility. Like the electricity in the wall socket, my service was always there. My lawns always looked great, too, for

I made it a point to exceed customer expectations, thus heading off complaints or even the need for contact. Most customers delegated lawn care entirely to me. Their only contribution was to pay the bill I sent them at the end of each month. Call me "Jim Edison."

You can go further. From referrals, I used to get phone calls requesting estimates. I'd check a lawn (usually at the crack of dawn) and call back later with a price. Often I'd get a go ahead ... and do the job weekly and bill it monthly for years on end — without ever meeting the customer at all!

Closing

The presentation, to repeat, is a soft negotiation. Don't dictate. Discuss. Find out what the prospect wants. Decide what you can do and for how much money. If there are differences, discuss the matter. See if you can isolate the problem and iron it out. The timing of the close is of some importance.

Don't try to close before you've reached general agreement on service and price. If you do, you may turn the prospect off. When you've reached general agreement, the prospect may close the sale for you: "Can you start this week, Mr. Adams?"

More likely, though, you'll have to initiate the close. "I'm in this area every Thursday, Mrs. Smith. If you like, I can put it on my Thursday afternoon schedule. Would that be agreeable?"

If she doesn't take you up on your offer, she probably "wants to think it over." As noted, that's either a mask for an objection or an excuse for not deciding right now. Sales books and training courses are long and strong on ways to overcome objections and close sales. Whole chapters are spent hammering away, twisting words, turning the prospect every which way but loose. Hard selling may have uses. But in what we're doing here, getting pushy probably does more harm than good.

Hard selling risks alienating not just one person, but also that person's neighbors, not to mention all the referrals the whole bunch might bring. You do not need negative publicity.

Objections sometimes involve issues the prospect doesn't want to discuss with you. For example, Mrs. Smith wants to hire you, but first she has to fire her no-account nephew ... and she's figuring out how to do it while keeping peace in the family.

Or consider this scenario: Mrs. Jones is on a really tight budget. This is the third estimate she's gotten for the job. The first guy came in really cheap, and she really has to try him ... but she has doubts about his reliability. Sure enough, he blows it, and you wind up with the job. This sort of thing happens fairly regularly. But it won't happen if you hammer prospects with high-pressure closes.

The point is that there are things you don't know, things people won't tell you. So when you hit an objection ("I need to think it over"), take it easy. Don't give up, just take it easy.

Go back over the things you've discussed. Is the money okay? The service? The terms? See if you can isolate the problem. Once the problem is isolated, you can use it as a close: "If I can put the job on my Friday schedule instead of Wednesday, Mrs. Smith, can we go ahead with it?"

Objections involving price are common. You'll go a long way toward resolving them if you make your "sticker price" (the first price you quote) somewhat high. That gives you room to back off. There's nothing to be gained by backing off easily, though.

When a prospect says it costs too much, don't get drawn into a nickel-dime haggling session. Instead, ask a question: "What do you think is a fair price for the job, Mrs. Smith?"

Suppose you quoted $30 per week to mow the lawn. Mrs. Smith says $25. You can almost certainly compromise at $27 or $28, which should be within your wiggle room. If even that's too much for her, you might point out to that $27 is only $2 difference ... only about $50 total for the entire season. If she's too cheap to go for that, you might not want this job so much after all.

Salesman that I'm not, I've resolved lots of price objections with a "try it" close that seems to work very well. "Mrs. Smith, I don't know how I'll come out at $27 per week. It seems low. But if it's agreeable with you, let's try it for a couple of weeks and see. I'll keep time on the job, and we can talk about it later. Okay?"

There's nothing to talk about later (surprise, surprise.)

Do a good job on her lawn. Get her hooked on your classy act. Charge $27 this season, $30 next season, $33 the next....

Paperwork

When making sales calls, take along a calculator, note paper, and proposal forms. You'll find proposal forms in the appendix. Other versions are available online, in office supply stores, or you can make up your own custom form.

As you run through your presentation, make notes of the prospect's needs and any special instructions. Whether you close the deal or not, at the end of the meeting rewrite your notes on a proposal form, also making a carbon copy. The prospect gets the original, you get the carbon. This is standard procedure for bidding commercial jobs. Even if you don't get the job immediately, carbon copies of bids are kept on file, as there's a chance of picking up jobs later.

For residential bids, many contractors use simple verbal agreements. But that's a mistake. Especially for anything at all complicated, you can avoid mistakes and arguments by putting it in writing. Even for the simplest job, a written proposal has advantages.

For one thing, it adds to your professionalism. It also increases the chance of picking up a job later if your initial bid is unsuccessful.

Should you try to hold customers to the absolute, legal letter of your formal proposal? Where money is concerned, absolutely. You provide your service in a timely manner and deserve to be paid the same way. With other matters, though, it doesn't pay to be too cranky.

5. Operations

What do you have to know to pass yourself off as a professional lawn mowing contractor? Not much. But you'll want to present a smooth, professional-looking operation from the first day. So, though much of what follows is common knowledge, I included it because it might be useful to someone.

Mulch or Bag?

When we started mowing some thirty years ago, we bagged grass clippings automatically. The matter was not discussed. That's the way things were done in those days, so that's what we did. Quite a few of our jobs were in upscale neighborhoods, with large lawns that were heavily-fertilized and irrigated. In one such neighborhood, people actually had grass-growing contests!

Do you know how much work these lawns are? Day in, day out, week after week, season after season, we spent countless thousands of grunty, sweaty hours loading reeking tons of grass clippings and driving them to the dump, where we unloaded them and — to add insult to injury — paid for the privilege. My stinking truck had a permanent cloud of flies that followed me everywhere. I remember the whole thing as a nightmare.

Today you see much less bagging. Most contractors mulch. You can buy mulching blades to fit just about any mower. Conventional high-lift blades work nearly as well, and the added lift sprays clippings over a wide area.

I strongly, strongly recommend mulching.

When mulching faster-growing lawns, some grass clippings may remain visible on the surface. Under these conditions it helps to mow the front yard first, then the back, then return to the front. By this time visible clippings should have begun to dry. Usually, mowing the area a second time on a different pattern will cause them to disappear.

If they don't quite evaporate ... so be it. Mulching — not bagging — was what you offered in the estimate. Your customers should understand that absolute perfection is not possible when lawns are growing fast.

A few customers don't agree. When we stopped bagging we lost a number of valued long-term customers. So be it. The remaining jobs were so much faster and easier, and required so much less labor and expense, that overall profits took a healthy jump.

Mowing

There are three things to know about mowing: Mowing height, mowing pattern, and blade sharpness.

Mowing Height

This depends on weather conditions. In the cool, wet periods common to either end of the season, excess moisture can cause lawn diseases. Grass should therefore be cut short, in order to aid drying.

In hot dry periods, conversely, the problem is not too much moisture but too little. Mower blades should be raised, leaving taller blades of grass to shade the roots and prevent them from drying out.

For recommended cutting heights and change dates, call local lawn fertilizing companies. Through the season in the Midwestern states, the usual range is from about 2 ½ to 3 ¼ inches. With tractors and other large-deck mowers, it's a good idea to set cutting height ¼ inch above the recommended level. Large-deck mowers tend to scalp, which means to cut high spots on the lawn too low. The added height reduces the problem.

Height adjustments found in an owner's manual are not to be trusted. To set height, wheel the machine onto a flat surface such as a sheet of plywood or a trailer deck. Check height with a measuring tape, by measuring from the flat surface up to the leading (sharp) edge of the blade. That's where the mower is actually cutting.

If you own mowers of different types, it's a good idea to check them all. To do this, run them one-by-one onto a flat surface. Adjust each machine through its full range, measuring actual cutting height at each stop.

Note the figures for that specific mower on a chart. From then on, when you decide to change cutting heights, you can adjust all your mowers to the same level without measuring anything.

Should you change mowing height lawn-by-lawn, at customer request? No. Tell customers that XYZ Fertilizing recommends this height and you feel you should use it. "Cutting shorter could damage your lawn, Mrs. Smith." Indeed it could.

Mowing Patterns

A professionally-maintained lawn should be pleasing to the eye. Pleasing appearance is achieved by producing the neat, striped effect seen on professional athletic fields. This is achieved by making parallel paths or "runs" across the yard, back and forth, slightly overlapping, with a 180-degree turn at the end of each run.

To cut any pattern, begin by mowing one or two borders around the area, for example the front yard. On the first border round, mow cul-de-sacs and other out-of-the-way areas completely, lest they be forgotten later. If you're using a side-discharge mower, on these initial rounds always discharge grass clippings to the inside, toward the middle of the yard. Never shoot clippings into decorative beds or against buildings or fences.

Once the border cuts are completed, start the pattern. Four patterns are commonly used: Parallel to the curb (or road), perpendicular to the curb, plus the two diagonals.

Parallel to the curb

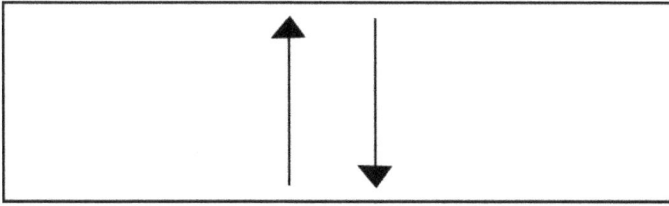

Perpendicular to the Curb

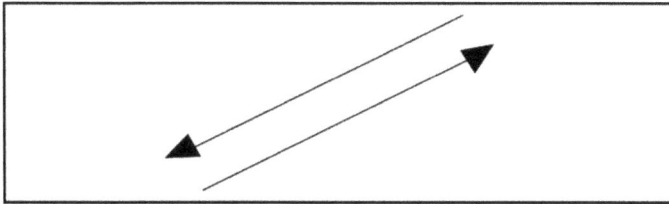

Near-left to far-right diagonal

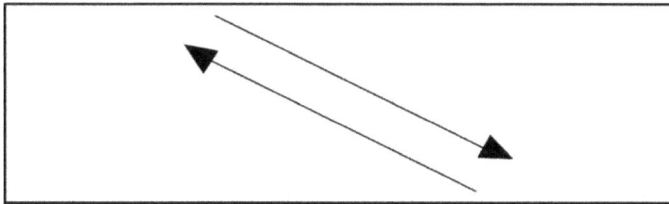

Near-right to far-left diagonal

In addition to these four patterns, three more can be useful. One is used for corner lots, and is simply an L-shape that follows the curb all the way. Another pattern is used on larger properties with S- (or otherwise-) curved driveways. Simply follow the curve and carry it out across the lawn. The appearance can be quite pleasing.

Finally there is one I call the "inside out" pattern. It's used when mowing heavily overgrown lawns. Using a side-discharge mower, cut two or three laps around the border in the usual fashion, blowing grass clippings toward the center of the yard. Then reverse directions. Turn the mower around so you are blowing grass clippings outward, into the just-cut border area.

Continue the same pattern, following round and round the border, spiraling slowly toward the center of the yard. If the going is heavy, cut about half a mower width at a time rather than a full swath. Also, run the engine and blades at full speed while traveling slowly over the ground. All this time you are blowing heaps of grass clippings to the outside. Thus do you scatter them as thinly and evenly as possible over the surface of the lawn.

A lawn cut in this fashion usually looks awful. Other than raking or bagging, there's not much you can do about it. The easy remedy is to wait a few days, until the grass clippings have dried and withered. Then mow again, using a conventional pattern. This second time over might still look ragged, but usually brings the lawn under control.

Back to conventional patterns. The two straight patterns — parallel and perpendicular to the curb — are cut by making straight runs back and forth across the lawn, slightly overlapping, with a 180-degree turn at the end of each run. The diagonal patterns are cut in the same fashion, though it is customary to start by cutting a baseline from corner to corner through the middle of the yard.

Once the pattern is finished, do not disturb. If your partner and his mower come out of the back yard and cut across your perfect front yard, shoot him. DO NOT DISTURB.

Transit the area by going around the border.

Generally, you'll want to mow each lawn on a pattern that looks good and is fast and easy to cut. Diagonals usually look good but are painfully slow. Usually the "favored" pattern is the one that allows for the longest runs across the yard and the fewest turns.

In the interest of efficiency, you'll want to use a lawn's fastest pattern much of the time. But that can cause a problem. Running the same pattern over and over can produce ruts that kill grass. This is especially true during wet periods or when using a heavy mower such as a tractor. If you're going to use the same pattern frequently, you can reduce ruts by offsetting the pattern by a tire width or two each week.

Blade Sharpness

A sharp blade cuts grass cleanly. A dull blade hammers its way through like a club, leaving ragged, "bloody" ends that are vulnerable to lawn diseases. Shortly after mowing, a lawn cut with a dull blade takes on a telltale grayish haze. Knowledgeable customers know this and will call you on it, so blades must be kept sharp.

How often should they be sharpened? Those who specialize in pampering luxury lawns sharpen blades every day. The rest of us sharpen once or twice per week.

Trimming

Trimming brings back memories that make me smile. In our early years in business we had a one-day route of thirty-some tiny lawns in an older section of Toledo where I grew up. We also had two big mowers run by high school linebackers. Those kids could mow one of those little postage stamps in minutes. I was the old gray trimmer. I learned to trim at jogging speed!

The secret to fast, efficient trimming is to get away from the hunt-and-peck routine. Don't trim something, raise your head and look around, go trim something else, walk backwards for a while, etc., etc.

Hunting and pecking is not only inefficient but requires thinking, which means one day you'll be distracted and miss something. Instead, trim each lawn according to a predetermined route. Fortunately, this is "one size fits all." With slight variations, the same route will cover every lawn you're likely to encounter.

The sketch on the next page shows the basic route. Notice that it begins and ends at the truck and includes everything on the property that might need trimming.

Notice also that as you walk this route, everything to be trimmed will pass by your left shoulder. This is for a person like me, who holds the business end of the trimmer off to his left. If you're more comfortable holding the trimmer the other way around, use this same route but walk it in the opposite direction.

FENCE

SHED

POOL

HOUSE

Start

TRUCK

When you trim a lawn for the first time, start by taking a moment to look it over. See how it fits the basic route. Adjust the route to fit this particular lawn, adding or subtracting loops as necessary. Once the adjusted map is in your head, that lawn belongs to you. No hunting or pecking EVER. You've put that lawn in a form of "muscle memory" — the same phenomena you use to drive to work without conscious thought and without suddenly finding yourself in Weehawken, New Jersey. In this mode, trimming is a quick jog along a familiar path, head down, feet moving fast.

Finishing

Finishing means blower-cleaning of walks and driveway, cleaning up any messes you've made, and checking your work to make sure it meets quality standards — yours, the neighborhood's, or the customer's — whichever is highest.

Additional Services

In addition to your main service, you'll be offered all sorts of odd jobs. Here are a few of them:

Sodding	Seeding
Dethatching	Soil aeration
Rototilling	Shrubbery trimming
Tree trimming	Shrubbery replacement
Tree removal	Fertilizing
Hauling	Irrigation
Gutter cleaning	Lot striping
Leaf cleanup	Spring cleanup
Landscaping	Blacktop sealing
Blacktop repair	Garage cleanup

Varied as it is, this list barely scratches the surface. The plain fact is, customers — senior citizens, in particular — have lots projects and the money to pay for them.

Plus which, because you're such a nice person, you can supply projects for those who lack them: "Mrs. Smith, your yard would look a lot better if we replaced those old shrubs with new ones."

With commercial accounts, a slightly different sales approach works well. Grounds managers are often on budgets, and they want to spend all the money allotted, lest the amount be cut next year. Want some of it? Ask for it: "Mrs. Smith, as soon as the money becomes available in your budget, we really ought to get those shrubs out back changed."

I know a guy who does this all day, every day. He has a big mowing crew that he stays close to all the time, and while they are mowing he is buttonholing owners, selling.

In my experience, you can sell all of this kind of work you can stand. As to the know-how to do various jobs professionally, you have two huge resources. One is the mother of all research tools, the Internet. I'm partial to Google. The other resource is your public library. I just checked the online catalog of our system (an excellent library for a mid-sized city.) On the topic of home improvement and repair I found eighty-eight titles. If you don't know your way around your library system, today is a good day to learn.

6. Efficiency

Suppose you've been in business five months. Sales are running about $800 per week. How much of that is net profit — yours to keep?

The answer depends on the efficiency of your operation. If you run a very tight ship — home-based, working alone, pinching every penny — you stand to net perhaps 70 percent of sales. You can't do much better than that, for fuel, repairs and other unavoidable expenses always take a bite. Still, 70 percent net profit is a outstanding return.

At the other extreme, sales of $800 per week could result in no profit whatever. You could spend every penny of it. And more. Big shot-types who sit home by the pool while hired help does the work can spend themselves right out of business.

If you want to make money, look to the efficiency of your business. Make sure you're getting the most out of every dollar you spend.

You'll probably meet contractors who think otherwise. A common notion in the lawn business is that bigger is better. More jobs, more machines, more troops — more of everything. And when that is not enough to earn good money, the solution is to get still more. One local contractor named Herb spent 20-some years patiently building his weekly volume to beyond $6000. Then he essentially gave his business to his foreman! Got himself a job applying fertilizer. Some people thought he'd lost his mind, but a few of us knew better. The fact is, his business wasn't making much money. It was so top- heavy with labor that it couldn't. All he was really doing was turning his hair white.

Now, this is not to say that there's anything wrong with growth. A business that grows and makes more money year after year is most gratifying. But bigger is not necessarily better. Better is better. A small, highly efficient operation will out-earn a big sloppy one every time.

Using Time Studies

As contractors, we commonly make decisions based on what seems to be true. A lawn that pays $80 per mowing seems a better deal than a lawn that pays $20, doesn't it? So, duh, we go for bigger lawns.

But of course that $80 lawn might take five hours and the $20 lawn only 20 minutes. That means the small lawn pays $1 a minute and the big one only 26 cents a minute. Duh indeed.

The purpose of time studies is to cut through the fog and get to the underlying reality. Instead of basing decisions on what appears to be true, you base them on what is true.

We mentioned an important time study, worker productivity, In the first chapter. Here's the formula again:

Gross income ÷ hours worked = $ per man-hour

Productivity numbers generated with this simple calculation indicate the profitability of your operation. The rule of thumb is that workers produce at least twice their wages (I'm happier with three times wages). If your workers aren't producing twice their wages, your slice of the profit pie is narrow indeed, if it has not vanished entirely. This is a problem to deal with immediately. Productivity numbers serve other functions as well. When you can measure profitability, you can isolate different portions of your business — a single job, a neighborhood, a work method, a worker or a crew — and determine which course is best. No more guessing, no more doing it the way you were taught, no more listening to your mower dealer or that goof from Toledo who wrote that book. With time studies, you can test various courses of action and find out which is most profitable in fact. Your business becomes more profitable because you base your decisions on facts.

Here are a few examples of questions you can answer with time studies:

Setting Prices: How much do you charge to mow a 12,000 square foot lawn? We've already discussed this, back in Chapter 3. But we didn't discuss how much to charge to trim a hedge or replace a shrub or ... well, hundreds of other odd jobs. The first time around on assorted jobs, you might not have a clue as to what to charge. So you might charge some lowly hourly rate that is acceptable to customers. But there's no reason to stay clueless. Keep time on every job you do. In short order you'll put together your own estimating book.

Evaluating Equipment: Which is more efficient, a 60-inch conventional lawn tractor or a 52-inch zero-turning-radius machine? Obviously, large items can't be bought just for test purposes. But they sure can be rented. Try it some time. Keep time on your jobs and routes as you mow them now. Then one day rent a ZTR tractor and see how much time it saves.

Comparing Neighborhoods: I used to enjoy working in older, blue-collar neighborhoods, among all those friendly retirees. But lawns were tiny and prices low. Were we coming out okay? Or should we try to expand on the few high-paying jobs we had out on the edge of town, in Big Bucks Acres?

I wasn't keeping time studies then, but Big Bucks certainly seemed better. Forty-buck lawns pay better than ten buck lawns, don't they? We went for it. Eventually we dropped the little stuff entirely. Just what we might have built for ourselves in that huge old neighborhood remains a mystery. But moving to Big Bucks turned out to be a mistake.

For we later came to realize, with the aid of time studies, that while luxury lawns paid a lot, it wasn't enough. Why? Two reasons, I think. First, stiff competition in upscale areas tends to depress prices. Second, big luxury lawns require lots and lots of labor. Labor, it turns out, that pays little. Eventually we discovered that downscale lawns are often more profitable than luxury lawns because they are so very quick and easy to do.

Which jobs, which routes, which neighborhoods in your business are most profitable?

Don't be misled by jobs that pay the most money. You want jobs that pay the most profit. Time studies will identify them.

Evaluating Employees: Suppose you're busy today, so you send out your crew — Bob, Carol, Ted, and Alice.

What do suppose those rascals are doing all day? Time studies will tell you if they had time to cut grass.

Comparing Work Methods: Suppose you have four jobs to do in four corners of town. Should you send your four-person crew to knock out one job quickly, then move on to the next? Or is it more efficient to split your crew up, sending one person out to peck away at each job? What is the optimum crew size for mowing a 15 acre apartment complex? What's the best way to handle leaves: Rakes? Blowers? Tractors with baggers?

You can think about such stuff till your head explodes and still come up with wrong answers. It's a whole lot easier to find answers with time studies. The two studies below will cover most situations.

Price Check

The price check is a time study designed to determine the profitability of individual jobs (or clusters of jobs) at single stops. Its focus is sharp and narrow.

To run a price check, start by listing the stops to be studied down the left side of a sheet of paper (spiral notebooks work well), along with the price for each stop. This can be done at home.

When you go to work, clock yourself "in" when you arrive at a stop and shut off the truck. Clock yourself "out" when you start the engine to leave. (I used to have a stick-on digital clock on my dashboard for this purpose.)

Note that no travel time is included in the price check. You want only the actual time spent at a stop.

Jot down start and stop times all day long. You can then complete the study at home with a calculator.

Determine the net minutes spent at each stop. If you are working alone, net minutes will be the actual time elapsed. If there are two of you, it will be double the elapsed time. Divide dollars the job pays by net minutes spent it to arrive at dollars (or, more likely, cents) per minute:

$35 ÷ 55 minutes = $ .64 per minute

What can you tell from the sample price check below?

Wednesday Route: Old South End

STOP	PRICE	TIME IN TIME OUT	NET MINUTES	$ PER MINUTE
Smith	$35	0800 to 0855	55	.64
Jones & Killer &- Roberts (3-job cluster)	$80	0905 to 1045	90	.88
Northville Apts.	$170	1045 to 0145	180	.94
Gregory	$15	0215 to 0245	30	.50
Archer	$18	0305 to 0340	35	.51
Lendle & Richards (2 jobs)	$45	0350 to 0605	135	.33

Obviously, the most profitable stops are the Northville Apartments, at 95 cents per minute, followed by the Jones cluster at 88 cents per minute. The poorest stop is the last one, Lendle & Richards, at just 33 cents per minute.

I can't tell you why some of these stops pay so much better than others. (Well, actually I can, because I'm making the numbers up as I write!) But you can tell, out there on the ground looking at the jobs.

Maybe you hate the apartments, because they are a giant sand pit that makes you feel like you've been sandpapered. Maybe so, but you're sure getting paid for it. And maybe you love the low-profit (under-priced?) Lendle stop, because it's a luxury condo that needs pampering, which is the kind of work you enjoy. Good thing, 'cause the money stinks.

Obviously, all of this has gigantic implications for your business. Types of jobs to seek, price increases, estimates — these things and many more are influenced by facts unearthed by price checks.

How much money should stops pay? Working alone, I liked a dollar a minute. That doesn't quite translate to $60 gross per hour, because travel time between jobs is not included, but it's nice territory.

But the best answer as to how much your work should pay comes from that great old labor union guy, Sam Gompers. One time he was locked in a lengthy, bitter negotiation. An exasperated company officer finally demanded to know what the hell he wanted. "More," Gompers said. Which, of course is exactly what the company wanted, too.

How much should your stops pay? More.

Route Check

The price check is for measurements relating to a single job or stop. The route check is for bigger fish — comparisons involving neighborhoods, routes, work methods, crew size and so on.

Timekeeping rules for a route check are to clock yourself "in" when you leave your base of operations in the morning and "out" when you return in the afternoon. Deduct for time taken for lunch and major delays such as thunderstorms, but include everything else — travel time, errand time, routine down time.

As to employee hours, if you work right along with your crew, count your own hours. If not — if you're mainly supervising, selling services to customers, and so on — exclude your own hours. Be as accurate as you can with this, or you'll skew the results.

The calculation for a route check is the same worker productivity calculation we've used before:

$388 gross income ÷ 16 1/2 man hours = $23.52 per man hour

This study is so easy, I suggest doing one every day. I kept figures for years, recording them on calendars that have a little square for each day (see below).

At the bare minimum, you'll want to note gross income for the day (work completed in dollars, whether you collected the money or not), worker hours, and worker productivity (WP).

Also note crew size and any other factor that might influence productivity, such as weather conditions, new machines, new employees, etc.

Monday	Tuesday	Wednesday	...
1 Income $ 255 Hours 14.5 Productivity $17.58 Crew 2	2 $360 11.5 $31.30 2	3 $236 11 $21.45 3	4
8 0 Rain all Day	9 (Monday Route) $240 15 $16 2	10 (Tuesday Route) $360 12 $30 2	11
15 $260 15 $17.33 2 Showers	16 $360 11 $32.72 2	17 $236 9 $26.22 2	18

What do these numbers tell you?

First, productivity on average is in the $20 to $30 range.

At today's prevailing wage rates that's livable, but certainly not great.

Second, notice the sharp variation between routes. The Monday route, at less than $20 per man-hour, is a dog. Tuesday at $30-plus is the best you have. Wednesday is so-so.

In my experience, some days are always markedly better than others. And there are always reasons. Perhaps Monday's route is made up of tiny, low paying lawns thinly scattered over a large area, so you spend more time riding in the truck than working. Perhaps Tuesday's route, by contrast, consists entirely of two large apartment buildings next door to each other, with no travel time between them.

Whatever the case, clearly you'll want to do more of the high-paying stuff you're doing on Tuesday and less of the low-paying stuff you're doing on Monday.

Can you do anything about that dog of a Monday? You can try. Crank in changes — different crew size, different methods, realigned routes — and keep an eye on the numbers. We did that once with a weak route and found that reducing the crew from three to two people caused an immediate leap in productivity. Go figure.

As the price check tells you which single jobs and stops are better than others, the route check tells you the same thing about larger parts of your business — routes, neighborhoods, work methods. Together, these two time studies tell you where your money is coming from.

Equally important, they tell you where it is not coming from.

Raising Productivity

Worker productivity translates directly to money in your pocket. So, no matter how respectable your numbers, higher is always better.

Figuring out how to raise worker productivity is what you do with your head while your body is cutting grass. Much of the content of the next chapter, a collection of tips and tricks, was hatched while bouncing along on a tractor.

Here are some obvious ways to raise productivity.

First, raise prices. If a $15 lawn suddenly becomes a $30 lawn, the person mowing it is suddenly bringing in twice as much money. Productivity has doubled.

Unfortunately, price hikes have a downside. Short of not showing up to do your job, jacking up prices arbitrarily is the surest way I know of to lose customers. As people come to know and value your service, they'll expect and accept modest annual price increases. These hikes definitely add up over time. But as a short term quick-fix, price hikes are not such a good idea.

A second way to raise productivity is a handmaiden to charging higher prices: Pay lower wages. One local outfit does this. They've had the same dismal crew of flunkies wandering around on sub-standard wages for decades. I do not know why.

There are a number of problems with substandard wages, but they all boil down to the fact that if you pay less you're gonna get less. Better people will stay only until they find better jobs, which never takes long. Only the flunkies will stay. Who wants to work with that gang? You're going to have to deal with turnover, inefficiency, increased training and supervisory expense, tardiness, absenteeism, inefficiency, bad attitudes, inefficiency — a whole range of problems found at the bottom of the barrel. There's enough of this on the high end of the scale, let alone stirring the sewer on the low end. It's better to hire and pay the best people you can find. Some of them will repay you in peace of mind and ... efficiency.

A third approach to increasing productivity is to crack the whip. Yell, scream, shout, threaten, fire ... maybe you've experienced this drill firsthand. It seems to work when the boss and the troops are in sight of one another, and maybe at other times as well. But this approach makes life so miserable for all concerned that it isn't even worth considering. So much for things that don't work.

Here are three approaches to raising productivity that do work.

1. Build on the Good While Eliminating the Bad

In all probability, your early advertising efforts will turn up a mixed bag of jobs. Good ones, bad ones, awful ones — we all go through this. Use time studies to sort them out. Find out where your money is coming from. Once you know that, aim your promotional efforts towards getting more of the same. Build on the good while reducing or eliminating that bad. Build on the good. That phrase applies to jobs, neighborhoods, work methods, employees, equipment — it applies to everything you do. Go where the money is. You'll put productivity on an uphill climb that never has to end.

2. Remove Bottlenecks

About 20 years ago, an unusual outfit mowed next door to us in a luxury neighborhood. A battered van would screech to a halt at the curb, every door would fly open, and five or six guys would jump out and go scurrying across the lawn like water bugs, each with a tiny push mower. In due time they'd all toss their mowers back into the van, jump in after them, slam the doors, and roar away. It was hilarious. I thought of them as Marx Brothers Mowing.

Unfortunately, the entertainment didn't last. They soon disappeared, as such outfits always do.

Why? Because those tiny, weak mowers were bottlenecks. They made even moderate productivity impossible. Even at a dead run, those kids could never cut much more grass than it took to pay their wages. The mowers just wouldn't let them.

Compare this with a the crew we use to mow big (ten acres and up) apartment complexes. It's just three people: two on fast ZTR tractors (see Chapter 9) and one trimming and blowing. It's built for speed, and commonly produces upwards of $200 per hour. That is profitable territory indeed.

Roofing with a claw hammer, sweeping driveways with a broom, painting walls with a brush — these are examples of bottlenecks. They choke productivity. To earn serious money, state of the art equipment is not a luxury but a necessity.

Bottlenecks take a number of forms besides equipment. Uncoordinated crew operations, clumsy and time-consuming equipment storage, unnecessary travel time — these and countless other bottlenecks ruin productivity. We'll discuss dozens of them in the next chapter. Suffice it here to say that you should examine your operation constantly. No matter how good it is, there's always room to make it better.

3. Develop a Culture of Productivity

Finally, the attitude of your employees is a key ingredient in worker productivity. If you accept a zombie-like hourly worker routine, with people doing as little as possible, then that's what you're going to get.

But suppose you run the best crew in town? This is a group that does first-rate work with unmatched speed, efficiency, and intelligence. A group that can handle any job . . . a group for whom nothing less that top performance will do.

WE'RE NUMBER ONE!!!

How do you build such a crew?

Your own attitude is the key. Be what you want your people to be — hard-working, innovative, enthusiastic.

Lead from the front. Don't yell at them, show them.

Trade publications are loaded with tips on building good crews. Top notch equipment and training, compliments for work well done, and various types of incentives are all parts of the deal. Employees who respond favorably will contribute to productivity not only in terms of physical work, but also by helping you find better ways to do things.

Let me conclude this chapter by returning to Herb, the contractor who gave his business to his foreman. His mistake was to pay too little attention to efficiency. He thought simple growth would make more money, so he grew and grew and grew. Eventually he reached a point where he was cutting massive amounts of grass in order to pay the expenses of cutting massive amounts of grass. Along the way, he created a nightmarish workload that finally beat him down. In the end, all he wanted was out.

Few of us go as far as Herb. But I'm convinced that the high rate of turnover among mowing contractors is caused by the same problem. You don't have to be a genius to set up a mowing business and make some money. But making the business better is not so easy. Most of us just make it bigger — more accounts, more machines, more troops. Before he did it himself, Herb told me many times that you can grow until you self-destruct.

As we grow our way to the moon and stars, we run afoul of a nasty little Catch 22. Efficiency is the key to profitability. But the bigger you get, the harder it is to be efficient. It gets much harder — the problems grow geometrically. So in trying to make more money you might actually make less. I think the self-defeating aspect of this, though largely unrecognized, has everything to do with the high rate of contractor turnover. You can get very tired of beating your head on the rocks.

Again, please don't get the impression from any of this that I'm against growth. Quite the contrary. But your numbers have to work. Bigger is not necessarily better. Better is better.

If your goal is to build a successful business, keep a close eye on productivity. That's the number that's controlling your income. When there's something wrong with it, don't ignore it or hope to outgrow it. Fix it.

7. Professional Tips and Tricks

Safety Rules

Every new piece of equipment comes with a list of safety rules. Read, understand, and follow these rules to the letter. In addition, here are some general rules that will help you to create a safe and efficient operation.

- Never mow steep hills with a tractor.
- Always wear eye protection when mowing, trimming, and edging.
- Always clear bystanders from the area when mowing, trimming, and edging.
- Never leave any machine with the engine running.
- Never work on a machine or touch any (potential) moving part without shutting off the engine and disconnecting the spark plug wire(s).
- Never use a machine for a purpose for which it was not designed.
- Never operate a machine without all safety guards in place.
- Never modify a machine in any way that increases revolutions per minute of impellers, blades, or other moving parts.
- Never design your own "blade boosters" or other moving parts, or install any parts except those supplied by a major manufacturer.

- If you work alone, take care to avoid personal injury, as even a minor scrape can cause serious difficulty. Analyze your work routine, identify hazards, and find ways to avoid them.

- Never put a new machine in service without reading and thoroughly understanding its special safety requirements.

- Note that you are responsible for enforcing safety rules among your crew members.

The Seasons

Here's an annual calendar of what to do and when to do it. (Dates are for the Toledo (Ohio) area, so you may have to adjust them.)

January and February

- Rebuild/repair all equipment as necessary. This is the time for maintenance projects.

- Shop till you drop. This is the time find out what's new.

- Submit bids on commercial jobs. Go for multi-year contracts by offering incentives such as no price increases through the period.

March and April

- Call all residential customers to confirm lawn service for the upcoming season. Ask about a spring yard clean-up. This call is the right time to raise prices by ten or fifteen percent. If you've been doing your job properly, most customers will accept it without complaint.

- Yard clean-ups (for methods, see "Handling Leaves," below.)
- April 15 to 20: Full mowing schedule begins.

October

- Grass growth slows. Leaf clean-ups begin towards the end of the month.

November

- Late in the month, finish leaf clean-ups and shut down operations for the year.
- Clean and winterize equipment and store it in a dry, secure location.

Handling Leaves

Fall leaf clean-ups, along with spring yard clean-ups, are considered a regular part of the job by most customers, so you really can't skip them. This is where a lot of school kids miss out. They think the season begins in June, when school lets out. Wrong. Here are some tips on handling these laborious tasks efficiently.

- When moving leaves, start by blowing them out of planting beds and away from buildings and other obstructions with a backpack blower.
- Once the leaves are out where you can get at them, the weapon of choice is a zero-turn tractor with a bagger. Sucking them up takes time — with leaves, everything takes time — but bagging with a tractor uses little labor and is therefore very efficient.

- Large, wheeled blowers are not the first choice. They move leaves well, but it's hard to stop them where you want them. On windy days you often blow leaves out one yard into another and wind up chasing them down the block.

- For limited leaf blowing, a side-discharge mower (walk-behind or tractor) is effective.

- In backyards with narrow gates "mowing in circles" is the method of choice. Using a side-discharge mower, mow 'round and 'round, blowing leaves inward, gradually tightening your circle. When the leaves (what little is left of them after repeated trips through the blades) are in a pile, bag them or rake them onto a tarp.

- When leaves will be disposed of by bagging or hauling, **always run them through a mower**. This chopping can reduce their bulk by an incredible 75% or more. Especially in dry conditions, the mower blades blast the leaves to shreds, a good portion of which trickle down into the turf and disappear.

Scheduling

- Agree to mow a customer's lawn on seven-day or fourteen-day intervals **only**. NEVER throw "ten day" lawns into the mix, or you'll soon be driving to all corners of the city every day.

- If a customer wants you to skip their lawn one week, it is their obligation to call you at least one day in advance. (You can't afford to drive around town with your crew, looking at lawns and discussing with customers whether a lawn needs mowing.)

- Even when the grass is short, never skip a lawn unless the customer asks you to. They might want it mowed anyway, because of an upcoming yard party or other event.

- NEVER share a job, i.e., you mow it sometimes and the customer mows it sometimes. This is a cheapskate dodge. When the grass is two feet tall, guess whose turn it is?

- NEVER accept "mow it only when I call you" jobs. More cheapskate dodge, more grass up to here.

- "Deluxe Mowing" (bagging of grass clippings, edging), if offered at all, is reserved for seven-day lawns **only**.

- Cut thin, weak lawns early in the day, as dew on these lawns is not a problem.

- Cut thick, fast-growing lawns later in the day, after the dew has dried.

- By law in many communities, residential lawns are not to be mowed before (usually) 8 or 9 A.M. To allow for crack-of-dawn starts, scatter commercial jobs through the week.

- When possible, avoid making special trips to a customer's house. When you have a few shrubs to trim or a similar minor job, do it on your regular mowing rounds.

- To allow for rain and other delays, limit your mowing schedule to 30 to 35 hours per week. If the schedule grows much beyond that, you need faster machines or more help. In a dry, trouble-free week, you should finish mowing no later than noon Friday.

- Customers who do not care when their lawn is mowed should be packed into the early part of the week.

- Customers who insist on late mowing (so it looks good for the weekend) should be eased back. Ease Thursday's jobs onto Wednesday, Friday's jobs onto Thursday, etc. Otherwise, in rainy periods, your week's work will spill into every weekend and even beyond.

- **NEVER** skip a lawn because of rain or other delays. If you pull up to Mrs. Smith's house on Monday just in time for a cloudburst, and it pours the next day too, when you come back to work on Wednesday, start exactly where you left off — at Mrs. Smith's house.

- Weather forecasts are more accurate about *what* is going to happen than *when* it will happen. Don't fall behind in your schedule because rain is hanging on the edge of the local radar. It's raining when you get wet, not before.

Routing

- To spread the working/driving balance through the week, arrange each day's jobs along a loop route that begins and ends close to home.

- When rain threatens, try to work the more distant part of the day's loop first. That way, if you do get rained out, the jobs missed will be close to home and easy to combine with the next day's route.

- Experiment with routes. Even if you know your area well, pinpoint your jobs on a map. Shuffle jobs and groups of jobs from one day to another, always looking to reduce driving time.

- Take a lesson from UPS: Limit left-hand turns. Some routes have you making left turns across six lanes of traffic all day. The same route run backwards may allow easy right turns. Experiment. Try cutting through the back streets. Find the easy way.

- When you pick up a new single job that is some distance from your usual route, evaluate it carefully. If it pays well, develop the area immediately. (See below.)

Judging the Turf

- NEVER mow once-a-year "lawns" such as vacant lots and fields. Hiding in those weeds are broken glass, rocks, and stumps that damage or destroy your machines.

- Even though you may not have a tractor for a while, it pays to center your business where lawns are flat and open — in other words, on tractor turf. Flat, uncluttered lawns are fast and easy with any sort of equipment. With a tractor you can fly.

- Weak, weedy lawns are often major money makers, as you can go really fast.

- If weak, weedy lawns in your area tend to burn out in hot weather, the remedy is to get more of them. Work overtime at the beginning and end of the season and go fishing in August.

Building Clusters of Jobs

- Time-study all jobs. Attempt to get more jobs in profitable neighborhoods immediately.

- Blanket the targeted neighborhood with flyers. Initial response may be disappointing, but don't be discouraged. People keep flyers for years.

- Be patient. Often, people have a "great" yard man ... and then one day he gets sent up the river. Then it's your turn.

- Get to know your competitors. Mutually beneficial job swaps can often be arranged.

- Offer your customers discounts for signing up neighbors. "If I had a couple more jobs, around here, Mrs. Smith, I could lower your price."

- Be friendly. Encourage neighbors to talk to you with a wave and a smile.
- Sometimes, vacation reliefs become permanent jobs. They are certainly worth cultivating.

- Reliability and quality of work are both important advertisements. Where you are trying to build up, keep your present lawns in the neighborhood looking extra-sharp.

- The ends of the season are excellent times to pick up new jobs. Weak competitors tend to start late in the spring and run for cover in the fall. Be the first one on your block to start and the last to shut down.

Wet Weather

- To disperse grass clippings when mowing in rainy weather, maximize the air stream coming off the mower deck. There are several ways to do this:

  - Run the mower engine wide open but move slowly over the ground.

  - Cut a narrow swath of grass.

  - Be sure the vane or "wing" area on the trailing edge of each mower blade is in good condition. If you mow over sandy soil, vanes wear out quickly.

- It's fine to take time off during rainy periods. But before you do, be sure all of your machines are in top condition, ready to go.

- When starting back to work after a delay, never skip ahead in the schedule. Pick up exactly where you left off.

- Don't accept being behind. Try to get back on schedule, working overtime as necessary.

- A lengthy delay can push your entire schedule into the latter part of the week. Move jobs back to their "right" days as soon as possible, even if this means mowing on an interval as short as four days.

- Never edge in wet weather. You'll only make a muddy mess.

Mowing Tricks

- Don't cruise around with the mower blades turned off. Especially on larger lawns, cut **something** all the time.

- All lawns have a "favored" pattern — that is, a pattern that is quick and easy to cut and makes the lawn look good. Usually the favored pattern is the one that allows the longest straight runs across the yard and the fewest turns. The favored pattern should be cut most of the time.

- Diagonal patterns are **never** favored. Too many short runs, too many turns.

- For lawns that are heavily obstructed — trees, shrubs, planting beds, etc. — try to find a pattern in which most of the clutter lines up like rows of trees in an orchard. Such a pattern will be favored, as fewer runs across the yard will be interrupted.

- When cutting the same pattern repeatedly, soil compacting (ruts) can become a problem. The solution is to offset the pattern by one or two tires widths each week.

- Don't disassemble yards to mow them. When faced with plastic flamingos and downspout extensions, mow and trim around them.

- When mowing moderate hills, always mow up and down the hill — never across.

- To avoid tipping the mower and possibly rolling it over, NEVER accelerate when climbing a hill. NEVER decelerate when going downhill.

- For maximum efficiency and profits, always use the largest, fastest mower available. Eventually this should be a zero-turn tractor. (See Chapter 9.) Much of what follows applies chiefly to tractors and other large-deck mowers.

- When driving a tractor, NEVER make turns on a hill. If there is no level spot at the top to turn around, the safe procedure is to roll back down the way you came up. Repeat this process — drive up the hill and roll back down, mowing all the time — till the hill is finished.

- When cutting a manmade hill, proper procedure is to cut it in two halves. Imagine the hill in cross-section; it will look like the letter "A" without a cross bar. Cut one side first. Mow parallel to the crest, the mower coming straight out of this page at you, the edge of the deck traveling along the peak of the A. Go around and cut the other side in the same fashion, the edge of the deck again traveling along the peak of the hill.

- Cut ditches the same as small hills. Imagine the ditch as the letter "V." Cut one side first. Mow parallel to the valley, the edge of the deck traveling along the bottom of the V. Go around and cut the other half in the same manner.

- **NEVER** cut across the crest of a hill. **NEVER** cut across the bottom of a ditch. These shortcuts risk damage to the lawn, to say the least. To get to the other side, always go around.

- Tractors and other large-deck mowers tend to scalp, that is, cut high spots too low. Scalping is reduced by cutting slightly higher than the recommended height. Usually, scalp spots can be cut with a large-deck mower, though you might have to try a several approaches to find one that works.

- Don't "prepare" lawns for tractoring by trimming them out with a small mower. You're wasting time. In experienced hands, a zero-turn tractor will cut almost anything, and do it with great speed and efficiency. It's in your interest to buy a first-rate tractor and learn to make full use of it. (See Chapter 9.)

- A tractor or large-deck mower not only mows but is also an effective blower. Use it for cleaning walks and driveways and moving leaves.

Trimming Tricks

- In normal operation, the trimmer is held so that the line spins parallel to the ground at the same height the grass is being cut.

- By elevating one side of the trimmer head so the line spins at an angle to the ground, debris will be thrown away from you. This is handy, for example, when trimming along a mulched bed. Mulch is thrown into the bed rather than out into the yard.

- By elevating the other side of the trimmer head, you can throw debris toward your shins. Though it really smarts, this technique is handy when trimming near objects that might be damaged, such as a basement window or a parked car.

- By twisting and turning the trimmer head to control the direction in which debris is thrown, you can trim along walks, steps, and patios and keep them clean. Thus a trip to the area with the blower is eliminated.

- With the string fully extended, the trimmer serves as a weak blower — handy for back walks and patios, as you'll save a trip with the blower.

- By turning the trimmer head so the line spins in a vertical plane, the trimmer serves as a light-duty edger.

- Careful mowing can reduce or eliminate trimming — it's always easy to trim when the people mowing are doing a careful job. The question is whether careful mowing is worth the time it takes. The answer is, careful mowing is worthwhile if it eliminates trimming in sizeable areas. If it only reduces trimming — if you're going to have to walk the area with the weed eater anyway — then careful mowing is a waste of time.

- Practice "two week" trimming: Trim a little lower than you should, to save steps next week.

- Commercial mowers will cut within a couple of inches of trees and other objects. Where it won't be too obvious, kill that last couple of inches of grass by scalping with the trimmer. You won't have to trim the area again for about per month.

- Trimming may also be eliminated by careful use of herbicide. Be sure to check with the customer and check applicable state and local regulations. Herbicides can get you into trouble.

- Trimming under fences can be eliminated by placing narrow strips of roofing material on the ground. Obviously, the customer's permission is needed.

- When you are the one doing both mowing and trimming, mow first. Make mental notes of what needs to be trimmed and what does not. Often you can save steps by the hundred.

Equipment and Supplies

- Do not use homeowner-style machines for commercial work. They're too slow and weak, and commercial use will almost certainly void the warranty.

- Never buy equipment from a non-servicing dealer. **YOU MUST HAVE DEALER SUPPORT**.

- Never pinch pennies when buying equipment. You want the fastest, the most powerful, the best. Top-notch machines pay for themselves dozens of times over.

- Your mower dealer knows which machines can take a beating and how to fix them when they break. Follow his recommendations.

- Your mower dealer may know a good bit about the commercial mowing business, and then again he may not. His opinions in matters discussed here should carry no special weight.

- Never buy cheap supplies. Cheap two-cycle oil fouls spark plugs and exhaust ports. Cheap trimmer line is so brittle it shatters and disappears by the mile. Products we specifically recommend are Echo or Tanaka trimmer line and Opti-2 two-cycle oil.

- Never use gasoline more than three weeks old in small engines. Dump it in the truck's fuel tank and start fresh.

- Due to condensation, the last few inches of gas in a can are often watery. If in doubt, pitch it.

Customer Relations

- Never work directly for a customer as if you were an employee. That is a dead-end position. Maintain your independence. You are a contractor providing a service for an agreed-upon price. All details are up to you.

- Two types of customers cannot be satisfied. Perfectionists think you've come to spend the day. Cheapskates think you and your crew and machines are worth maybe $3 an hour. Such people cannot be reformed. If they're causing trouble, move on.

- When quitting a job, always quit gracefully. "Sorry, Mrs. Jones, but things aren't working out for me here. I'll take care of it for now, but please find somebody else."

- **Never** raise prices arbitrarily during the season. Customers who are satisfied with your service will happily accept a moderate price increase each spring, but the increase should result from friendly negotiation.

- When you're just getting started, you might want to collect your money as you finish each job. But it's more professional and more efficient to use a monthly billing system. Don't pester Mrs. Smith for money every week. Don't destroy your own productivity by standing on the porch while she hunts up her pen, then her checkbook, then another pen that might work, then a calendar….

8. High-Efficiency Lawn Mowing

T his chapter takes one last look at efficiency, this time as you see it — or fail to see it — on the job. Most people think a crew is the best way to go. I think they're the worst. Why?

Troubles with Crews

- Three guys come to work in the morning, but the fourth — desperately needed — fails to show. So you sit and wait and sit and wait, not knowing he's in jail.

- A four-person crew hauls four times as many people from place to place as a one- person crew. Travel time pays nothing, so that's a four-to-one-loss. And because the big crew does jobs so quickly, it must move more often, covering great chunks of real estate in a day. I don't know how to calculate it, but the total loss here is enormous.

- The job is all but finished when Mike, bless his malevolent soul, rips the cord out of the only blower. Three people take a nap while you make emergency repairs.

- The new guy, Archie, is a little slow. Older crew members resent having to do what they see as his work. So they back off to match his pace.

- Unless you haul a fleet of ZTR tractors around, on many lawns grass by definition is mowed with machines too small for the job. A 60-inch

ZTR tractor cuts roughly ten times as much grass as a 36-inch walk-behind, so the loss here is enormous.

- As a professional, you should be the most productive person on the crew — best tractor driver, trimmer, and so on. But your day is spent supervising slower people. Your exceptional experience and productivity produce ... nothing.

In short, crews are inefficient. I'll show you why.

Case Study

We're going to mow the same lawn twice. The first time, we'll use a three-person crew. Then we'll mow it again using just one person, the crew leader.

The lawn is a suburban home site of nearly two acres, five miles off our regular route. It has a house, driveway, pool, planting beds, manmade hill, a ditch across the front, and a section of rail fence out back. It pays $100 per mowing. That might be on the cheap side for this pricey neighborhood. But we're new here, trying to pick up more jobs, so we're holding prices down.

Mowing with a Crew

People: You are working along with your crew, Bubba and Sissy.

Machines used: 36-inch walk-behind mower, 60-inch zero-turn tractor, trimmer.

The first thing to notice is that it takes 20 minutes to get to the job from our regular route. So we're paying our crew — Sissy and Bubba — $6 to ride to the job, and another $6 to get back on our route later. That's $12 — twelve percent of what the job pays — spent riding.

Both Sissy and Bubba are fairly new. Unfortunately, new people in the lawn business are the norm. Employee turnover has been a massive headache for years if not for decades. We pay a price for it. Among other things, turnover means that your crew won't function like the proverbial well-oiled machine you dream about. Much of the time, in fact, it creaks along with parts that don't fit or are missing entirely.

And that's too bad. Because when you think about it, the owner, the crew leader — you — are the most experienced and productive person in sight. You are, or should be, the best tractor driver, the fastest trimmer, and so on. But your exceptional productivity counts for little because you spend most of your time directing others.

You — the fastest, best one-third of your crew — produce far less than you could. It's impossible to put specific numbers on the loss here, but it has to be enormous.

Meanwhile, back on the job....

Because she is careful, Sissy has become the designated trimmer. She's not fast — she spends countless long seconds patiently gunning down single weeds — but at least she misses nothing. That's important, for it means you don't have to walk in her footprints all day.

Besides which, on this job, trimming speed seems unimportant. You and Bubba have about an acre and a half to mow, so Sissy has a heap of time for the little bit of trimming needed here.

You're going to run the 60-inch tractor, Bubba the 36-inch walk-behind mower. Too bad you don't have another tractor and too bad Bubba doesn't know how to drive one yet. Too bad because the loss in efficiency here is huge. Think about this: Bubba's mower, the 36-inch walk-behind, running at walking speed (3 mph) cuts about an acre of grass an hour. The tractor, which is wider and much faster (ten mph), cuts nearly six acres an hour.

That's an enormous difference.

By using the 36-inch walk-behind, you're cutting part of this big lawn at less than 20% of available speed and efficiency. That's awful. Yet for many outfits it's standard operating procedure. I see it every day. But there's nothing we can do about it at the moment.

So off we go, you on the tractor headed for wide open spaces, Bubba to the front ditch and the little manmade hill, these areas being better suited to his smaller mower. You see that Sissy is headed for the back fence and trees, a change of trimmer line peeping from her hip pocket, as instructed. Good. On larger lawns you never want to range far from the truck without spare line.

Hmmmm, you wonder. Do the back fence and trees need trimming this week? You aren't using herbicide on this job. You told Sissy to scalp all the outlying areas with the trimmer last week. Did she do it? Should you zip out back on the tractor and see? Maybe save Sissy some steps? No. That would be a waste of tractor time. So you let her continue on her way, going to trim what probably does not need trimming at all.

Meanwhile, out front, Bubba has stopped. He's waving his arms to get your attention. Your heart rises into your throat. You shut down the tractor blades (now both mowers are out of production) and go see what he wants.

Uh-oh. It turns out that he ran over the crest of the little hill and scalped it. You're looking a square yard of bare dirt. @#%$#*&^//?%=!!!!!

Oh well, you think, the small black cloud over your head slowly drifting away on the breeze ... Bubba is not exactly a rocket scientist. You don't hire a whole lot of rocket scientists in this business. You'll have to fix the lawn, that's all. Next week. Bring a little black dirt, grass seed, water, straw, a rake. Better tell the customer about it today, though. You don't want her to think you've damaged her lawn and are trying to get away with it.

Strong instructions to Bubba ... and back to work we go.

Uh-oh. Sissy isn't at the back fence, but is heading for the truck. Now what? Did something break? You slow down and watch her.

No, it's nothing ... no big deal. The trimmer just ran out of gas, that's all. You make a mental note **again** to remind Sissy **again** to gas the trimmer before each big job.

She's doing okay, though. At least she doesn't gas the trimmer on the lawn, and spill gas and kill the grass (something **else** to fix.) Good old Sissy. In minutes she's headed for the back fence, to finish trimming what probably does not need trimming.

For some minutes you mow in peace. Then Bubba disappears into the ditch — all but his head — and stops. You stop too. Two machines sitting still again. Did his mower stall or get stuck?

No. Bubba's head bobs around and starts on its way again. Presently he and his mower emerge from the other end of the ditch. Another crisis averted. You make a mental note to cruise by the area and see what, if anything, he did to the turf.

So it goes. Eventually Sissy finishes a one-mile trimming route, most of which could have been skipped. Bubba spends an hour mowing his part of the lawn. You spend an hour mowing a much larger part.

This is easily twice as long as it should take, but that's because much of your attention is focused on your crew.

At least we're almost done. You check the ditch for turf damage, then blow off the long driveway with the tractor, then pull onto the trailer and shut down. While Bubba and Sissy load and secure equipment for travel, you walk up that long driveway to the house to tell Mrs. Jones about the scalp spot you'll repair next week.

Ring, ring. Wait. Try knocking. Knock some more, wait some more. The clock ticks on. She doesn't appear to be home. You walk around the house and ... there, on the back patio. Grass clippings.

Bubba did it — no one else could have. He made an amateur turn and blew grass clippings onto the patio. @#%$#*&^//?%=+0!

If you make a mess, you have to clean it up. (Duh.)

Bubba's blunder has resulted in a law: Jim's First Law. It should be written on the inside of every mowing contractor's eyelids: *Don't make a mess and you won't have to clean it up.*

Actually, this boo-boo is your fault. You should have checked the patio yourself, while still on the tractor. Usually, tractors aren't good for blowing off patios — too many obstructions — but at least you would have known and might have saved a little time.

Now ... back down the long driveway you go.

Sissy and Bubba are resting beside the truck. You tell Sissy — trustworthy Sissy — to take the blower and blow off the patio. The blower is out of gas. After refueling, Sissy heads up that long driveway.

Meanwhile, you give Bubba additional instruction on turning his mower so it blows grass away from the patio, then write yourself a note to call Mrs. Jones tonight.

Eventually the job is done.

We've been here just over an hour, plus travel time. How did we come out? Though the time seems a bit long, Bubba and Sissy have been fairly consistent lately, producing just about three times their wages. On that basis you'll net maybe a third of what this job pays.

Call it $34. This for perhaps one and a half hours of your time.

Now let's regrow the grass and mow it again.

High-Efficiency Lawn Mowing

This is going to be a short section because this is a short job.

People: You are working alone.

Machines used: 60-inch zero-turn tractor, trimmer.

It takes you 34 minutes to mow the entire lawn. This is easily within the capability of the tractor. Except for brief slowdowns for the ditch, the hill, and a few other obstructions, you run flat-out the whole time. No rubbernecking at your crew here: The job at hand has your full concentration.

While you are mowing, you make mental notes of what needs trimming and blowing. This is very important.

You're not just going for a tractor ride, however relaxing that might be. You are looking all the time, seeing what needs to be done.

Your time is too valuable to miss things and have to go back and do them later — too valuable, too, to be spent fixing boo-boos or fielding customer complaints. So everything is checked every week.

On this particular lawn, since you scalped with the trimmer two weeks ago, most of it still looks good.

There's only a little trimming to do, right around the house. (On very large lawns, it's a good idea to carry the trimmer along on the tractor, so you don't have to walk to outlying areas later.)

Working alone saves a world of time.

No need to stop, get Sissy's attention, explain to her what needs trimming and what does not.

No need to communicate at all. When you work alone, communication and instruction — huge time-consumers in crew operations — are eliminated.

Five Keys to Maximum Efficiency

1. Work alone (no communications.)
2. Cut everything with a zero-turning-radius commercial tractor (no small mowers.)
3. Mulch grass clippings — do not bag them.
4. Make full use of pro tips and tricks. (See chapter 7.)
5. Mow only high-profit lawns, as identified by time studies. (See chapter 6.)

Back to work. You finish mowing and blow off the driveway with the tractor. No need to check the back patio for grass clippings ... you haven't made an amateur, Bubba-style turn since 1955.

So one quick lap around the house with the trimmer and you're done.

Total time for the job: 48 minutes.

Since you have no payroll, the rule-of-thumb says you'll net about 70% of what the job pays: About $70 for about an hour of your time.

Fantasy? No. This is what I did for a living for over a decade.

A Few Observations

The lawn we mowed in this chapter is real. It's on a golf course ten minutes from where I sit right now. I mowed it weekly for 16 years. We also mowed similar lawns in the area for varying periods.

We did them all different ways — both bag and no-bag, with a variety of machines, with big crews, small crews, and no crews. The elimination of bagging, needless to say, brought a healthy increase in productivity and profits. So did the elimination of the crew.

Getting slow machines and slow people off these big lawns made a huge difference. So did the elimination of supervision and communication, both of which are major bottlenecks.

Working alone obviously has advantages. Unfortunately, it has drawbacks as well.

Chief among them is that it limits the growth of your business. You make easy money, but there's definitely a ceiling. I'm not prepared to say just what that ceiling is, but there has to be one somewhere.

I started working alone mainly because I was tired of babysitting Bubba and Sissy. At that time, we didn't have enough large lawns to keep me busy. But clusters of smaller lawns do just as well. In Toledo, there are hundreds upon hundreds of these lawns and little competition for them.

A group of small lawns pays as much as one big lawn.

The chief problem with smaller lawns in older neighborhoods is narrow backyard gates. I got around this in some cases by changing gates or getting customers to change them. I also gained access by dropping fence rails. I also lost some accounts.

Easy come, easy go. In recent years I've seen increasing numbers of small zero-turn tractors, designed for smaller lawns. It seems to me that there's an excellent opportunity here, as a "smaller lawn" specialist working older areas of the city. If you are using one of these small tractors, or thinking about it, I'd like to hear from you.

Anyway, that's high-efficiency mowing in a nutshell: An experienced pro on a fast tractor, working alone, using every trick of the trade, going like hell.

NO HELPERS. NO SMALL MOWERS.

This was my M.O. for over ten years. The challenge is to see how many tricks you can dream up and apply, how fast you can go, how much money you can make. Thus do you turn the ho-hum business of mowing lawns into something of a sport.

Finally, let me offer a comment on the rather bumbling mowing crew above, with Bubba and Sissy. Was that a fair depiction? Yes and no. Sometimes you luck out and get a couple of good, smart kids who last a whole season. What a great time that is! But then there are all those other years....

9. Equipment

When my son and I went into business in the early 1980s, we started with two garage sale mowers and a quart jar of bartending tips. The machines didn't last and neither did all those dimes, but then they shouldn't be expected to.

In commercial use, you put about 30 years of wear on a machine in a single season. Homeowner stuff isn't built — or warrantied — for such hammering. The result is frequent breakdowns, difficult repairs, and short life span.

But that's only half of it. Few homeowner machines are fast enough to earn serious money. Poor machines have you working harder and earning less.

So ... start where you must, as we did. But be ready to move up to commercial equipment quickly. Mower dealers know that fast machines pay for themselves quickly, so terms are generally liberal.

For further information about the types of machines described here, see the Appendix at the end of this manual. You'll find a list of about sixty equipment manufacturers.

Use the links not only to compare machines but also to find sales, closeouts, and other deals. Often these are offered in late winter and spring, and you can find some tremendous bargains. Most of these sites steer you into the company's dealer network. Remember, you're going to need a LOCAL dealer to supply parts and service, including warranty service.

Walk-Behind Mowers

The commercial walk-behind is the first step up from homeowner mowers. For years these familiar machines have been the backbone of the mowing industry. Simple, versatile, tough, reliable, reasonably fast, stable on hills — this is the go-anywhere, cut-anything mower. Standard width is 36", though wider and narrower decks are available.

Commercial walk-behinds have two drawbacks.

One is that speed is limited to walking speed. The other is that operator fatigue is high.

On large lawns, both problems can be reduced somewhat by adding a sulky, which is a small trailer on which the operator rides.

Today, commercial walk-behinds, like cars, are offered in various configurations, from bare-bones versions to deluxe machines with all manner of bells and whistles.

Bare-bones machines are less troublesome. Beyond that, we have no specific recommendation. Buy what your mower dealer promises he can keep running.

Stand-Up Riders

The stand-up riders made quite a splash when they hit the market a few years ago. And well they should have, for they promised to retain the versatility of the walk-behind while achieving the speed of the zero-turn tractors (discussed below.)

Like most compromises, stand-up riders fall short of perfection. For example, you can't tip them up on edge and drag them through narrow gates as you can a walk-behind, nor are they as handy at hopping curbs to mow islands.

They won't give you the all-day-long speed of a tractor, either, as operator fatigue is simply too high.

All that said, stand-up riders definitely have a place. Speed is greater than that of walk-behinds, and stand-ups are safer on hills than tractors.

Price-wise they fit midway between walk-behinds and tractors. If any or all of these factors are important, the stand-up could be your best choice. Beyond that we have no recommendations. Buy what your mower dealer can keep running.

Zero-Turn Tractors

Zero-turn tractors are the Cadillacs of the mowing business. If you're not familiar with them, these are riding mowers that are controlled by means of a pair of levers — the same system used on bulldozers.

Control is easy. Push the right lever forward and the right drive wheel rotates forward. Pull the same lever back and the wheel turns backward. The left side works the same way. The further you push the levers the faster the wheels spin.

To make a turn, counter-rotate the drive wheels by pushing one lever forward and pulling the other back. The machine pivots to a new heading.

This is NO turning radius. Hence the term "zero-turn" or ZTR, both short for "zero turning radius."

Compared to conventional tractors, zero-turns are expensive. It's worth asking why you should pay the high price of such a machine. The answer is speed. Productivity. Zero-turn tractors earn more money than other types of machines.

Money, as we've said repeatedly, comes from speed. But mowing speed is limited by three factors.

One is speed over the ground. Speed over the ground is normally limited to ten or twelve miles an hour. Beyond that, on most lawns the mower bounces too much to cut evenly (or, for that matter, stay aboard).

A second limiting factor is deck width. The wider the deck the more it cuts, but also, on the downside, the more it scalps. Plus which wider decks might not pass through backyard gates, between trees and so on.

So we have two limiting factors: over the ground speed of ten or twelve mph and deck width — depending on where you work — of perhaps 50 or 60 inches.

The third limiting factor is maneuverability. This is where the zero-turns truly shine. Conventional tractors are clumsy beasts, requiring turning, stopping, shifting gears, backing and filling, and so on. They're just plain slow.

When buying commercial mowers, you'll often have a choice of engines. Always buy the biggest engine available. In tough conditions — rain, overgrown lawns, wet leaves — you'll appreciate the extra horsepower and be glad you spent the money.

In easier conditions, when a small engine might still be pushing near its maximum, the big engine will be loafing along at cruising speed. Other things being equal, it should last far longer.

By comparison, a zero-turn absolutely flies. And in experienced hands it will cut practically anything — moderate hills, ditches, humps, ridges, within inches of trees, bushes, buildings and other obstructions — practically anything. Control is so precise that you can often eliminate trimming.

And operator fatigue is low. I bounced around on a ZTR all day long till I was well into my sixties. (I think I'm quite a bit shorter than I used to be, but there's no free lunch.)

Need I tell you I am sold on zero-turns?

Years ago, there were only a couple of ZTRs on the market. But because they are money-making machines, demand has skyrocketed, and supply right along with it.

Today there are dozens of brands and models. Some of the differences between them are mere bells and whistles, and you know how I feel about that stuff. But there are substantive differences as well. Here are several:

Established Manufacturer

In the rush to get into the zero-turn market, a number of fly-by-night outfits have popped up. These outfits tend to disappear and take their spare parts with them. Check with your mower dealer. Buy a machine built by an older, well-established company.

Dual hydrostatic Drive

Some machines achieve zero-turn capability by means of special transmissions or mechanical devices, and some of them are admittedly ingenious. But that's homeowner stuff. For day-after-day commercial hammering, the tractor needs dual hydrostatic drive. Make sure that's what you get.

Direct Drive

Years ago at least two leading manufacturers sold tractors in which the drive system amounted to a bewildering bird's nest of chains and sprockets. Avoid such stuff. You're only buying things to fix.

Buy a tractor in which the hydrostatic pumps drive the motors and the motors drive the wheels. Period.

Deck Placement

Some tractors have the mower deck mounted out front, in the manner of a walk-behind. On others, the deck is suspended from the frame below the driver's seat (more or less), a configuration called a "belly deck".

Which is preferred? I like the belly deck because the overall machine is more compact, an advantage in smaller yards. But front decks have advantages too, such as nosing under low-hanging trees without ripping your face off.

Such are some of the things to look for when buying a zero-turn tractor. Beyond that, buy what your mower dealer can keep running.

String Trimmers

The weed eater, or string trimmer, is an important production tool. I can't count the times I've seen an entire crew held up, twiddling its collective thumbs, while one person fiddles with a troublesome trimmer. This is expensive fiddling.

So it pays to buy a first rate "pro" model trimmer ... or two of them, for instant back-up. Many companies offer first-rate machines. Echo is popular in these parts.

When shopping for a trimmer, there are a couple of things to avoid. One is an automatic line feed. These systems work fine until they get beat up and dirty. Then they give you fresh line on their schedule, not yours.

Also avoid curved shafts. There are two problems here. One is that the "knee" of the shaft is forever in the way when you are trying to trim under fence rails, low hanging shrubs, etc. The other is that that same "knee" puts that spinning, nasty string dangerously close to your toes. That's a pain you will not soon forget.

The proper machine will have a long, straight shaft and a bump-feed head. The head swings two strings that are .095 inches in diameter. Overall, the machine is light, well- balanced and powerful.

Edgers

On most commercial jobs and in upscale neighborhoods, edging of walks and driveways is expected. Frequency is negotiated when the estimate is done, and might vary from once per week to once per month. Avoid longer edging intervals, as overgrown edges make for a long, ugly, sweaty job.

If you're going to use your edger constantly, a heavy-duty "pro" model is recommended. Tanaka builds a real bear — the best edger (and arguably the best machine) I've ever owned. Little Wonder has a good one too. These top-of-the-line edgers last indefinitely, but they are very expensive — about what you'd pay for a bad used car.

If you work in mid-scale neighborhoods, you'll edge less, and can probably get by with an inexpensive homeowner model. In some of the places we used to work, you didn't need an edger at all, though body armor wasn't a bad idea.

Let me add a word about a newer critter on the block, namely the stick edger. This machine is a weed eater with an edging head. I am told that they are too weak for heavy work and that they wear out quickly. On the plus side, they are light, quick, and handy. All things considered, a stick edger would not be my first choice.

Blowers

Blowers come in three styles: hand-held, backpack, and wheeled. As with edgers, the type of blower you'll need is determined by the work you do.

Hand-held blowers

Looking something like guitars, these little machines are great for quick residential clean-ups. (The real secret to blowing is, don't make a mess in the first place, and you won't have to clean it up. Duh.) Plus which the little blowers are so cheap that expensive repairs are never needed. You just throw one away and buy another. I went through four or five eighty-buck blowers in twenty-some years and see it as a bargain.

Wheeled blowers

If the little hand-held blowers are handy, wheeled blowers are the downright cumbersome. Ranging from five to eight horsepower, these big machines have the power to clear parking lots and move whole yards of leaves. But for general clean-ups of residential and smaller commercial properties, they're slow and fatiguing ... it's like dragging around a tank. Not recommended.

Backpack blowers

For general clean-ups of larger residential and most commercial jobs there really is no contest. The backpack wins going away.

I despise backpacks. They cling to your sweaty body and scream in your ear, and are awkward to climb into and out of. They're easy to break and harder to stow away on the trailer than an octopus.

But the thing is, the more powerful backpacks have just the right amount of power for larger residential and smaller commercial jobs. The little hand-held blowers are too weak and the wheeled blowers too clumsy. Like Mama Bear's porridge, the backpacks are just right, even when cleaning up after a messy edging, even for moving moderate amounts leaves.

Buy the most powerful version offered. Beyond that, follow your mower dealer's recommendation.

Trailers

Years ago, for about one season, I mowed lawns next door to a contractor who was not, shall we say, the sharpest blade on the block. He had a large equipment trailer which, when hitched to his truck, assumed a sad, nose-down posture, with the tail end about armpit high.

He didn't have a ramp, but ran his machines up and down a pair of planks. About half the time he didn't make it. A plank would kick out, sometimes bounding across the yard like a giant boomerang, while the machine crashed to the ground. When he was loading up, I always found something to do behind the house.

If that nitwit is still alive and has all of his body parts, it's no fault of his own. There's no surer way to hurt yourself, your crew members, and your expensive equipment, than with an inadequate trailer.

With trailers, it's *safety first*. And, oddly, it's *productivity second*. For a trailer is a key production tool. You might load and unload it twenty times a day, and every second is job time. So it's worth considerable time and effort to make your trailer not only safe, but quick and easy to use as well.

Proper equipment trailers are available at countless outlets including Lowe's and Tractor Supply Company. Many welding shops also fabricate trailers. Prices vary hugely, so it pays to shop around. For beginner or high-efficiency operations a single axle is adequate. For larger crew-type operations, a tandem axle is recommended.

The right trailer will have a full-width hinged rear ramp made of non-slip material such as expanded sheet metal.

When hitched to the truck, the tail of the trailer will be less than eighteen inches from the ground. This combination of a wide ramp and a low tailgate assures safe, easy loading and unloading of machines, even in the rain, even when everything is slick with grass clippings.

Avoid snowmobile-type trailers with small wheels that fit under the deck. We had one briefly. Then one day as I accelerated onto a road near home, I felt a tug and heard a screech. I looked in the mirror just in time to see one of those small wheels that fit under the deck disappear into a nearby cornfield. @#%$#*&^//?%=+0)!!

Sometimes, I see people roping machines down as if they were moth-balling the *Queen Elizabeth II*. Spare me, Lord.

 Tie-downs even for large machines can be quick and easy. With my simple rig, I found it handy to drive my tractor up against the front rail of the trailer and secure it with a single heavy nylon strap. The small stuff — weedeater, blower, gas cans, trimmer line, tool box — ought not to be floating around loose on the trailer deck, where it can get crunched.

Many contractors build a tray for small stuff across the front or down one side of the trailer. Security is always an issue, so some sort of lockup arrangement needs to be provided. Early on, we used bicycle cables with locks. Later I drove a pickup truck with a cap, and kept the little stuff inside.

Finally, these days, I see increasing numbers of enclosed trailers. From a security standpoint, the advantage is obvious. Outside of that, I see only drawbacks. On the job, they can't be as quick as an open trailer, where every crew member can grab a machine and go. And gas stops look positively painful. Recently I watched a guy wander in and out of the dark interior of a large trailer with a five-gallon gas can, patiently refilling it at the pump, then (presumably) dumping it into a mower. Efficiency nut that I am, I wanted to smack him and make him stop it.

Here's another drawback: On a ninety-five-degree day, wearing shorts and a tee shirt, I really don't want to go clambering up in that dark trailer among all those burning hot machines to make some minor repair. I don't want to unload everything, either.

All things considered: no thank you.

Maintenance

My first tractor was a 52-inch ze ro turn that cost about $4,500. It lasted for six years and cut about $240,000 worth of grass. That's over fifty times its initial cost, a bargain if ever I saw one.

Getting that return took a good deal of work, of course, not to mention expense in the form gas, oil, tires, a new engine, batteries, and general repairs. I broke the frame a dozen times; toward the end, I had welded so much iron on it that it was getting awfully heavy. But the point remains: quality equipment pays for itself many, many, many times over.

Not so the cheap stuff. It breaks often and can be difficult or impossible to repair.

So the first rule under "maintenance" is to buy first-rate equipment. The second rule is to maintain those expensive machines to manufacturer's recommendations or beyond.

Dirt is **the** major enemy of small engines. It gets in through or around the air filtration system and mixes with the engine oil, turning it into a liquid grindstone that causes severe wear. Make sure all air filters are clean and properly sealed. In dry and dusty periods, air filter maintenance is a daily job.

Preventative Maintenance

Manufacturer's recommendations will be found in the literature that comes with the machine. READ AND FOLLOW THE INSTRUCTIONS RELIGIOUSLY.

Usually, machines with two-cycle engines (trimmer, probably the blower, maybe the edger) need little maintenance. A drop of oil or grease here or there, cleaning, regular changes of air filters — that's about it.

Mowers need more attention. The manufacturer might recommend checking the engine oil, greasing the blade spindle bearings, and cleaning the air filter every day. Less frequently, perhaps once or twice per week, you'll need to sharpen blades, grease all fittings, and change engine oil and filter.

Vee belts used on commercial mowers are very expensive at mower shops. At *belt* shops they are typically less than half price. See "Belting and Belting Supplies" in the Yellow Pages.

Will you remember to do all this stuff on schedule? Or should you make up a "Master Maintenance Schedule" and keep detailed written records?

If you need it, by all means, make up a schedule. At one time, we kept elaborate records. I listed all maintenance chores and their frequency down the left side of a spiral notebook page, then noted the dates the jobs were done on that and the following pages. Some jobs, such as air filters, were checked every day and cleaned as necessary.

> Popular notions to the contrary, air- cooled engines do have cooling systems. The typical system starts with an impeller mounted on the flywheel. The impeller sucks in fresh air and, guided by cowlings, blows it over cooling fins on the heads. When doing leaves or other "dirty work," these air ways often become clogged, resulting in overheating. Check cooling systems regularly.

Later I got away from written records in favor of an informal system not unlike a morning bathroom routine. You don't forget to brush your teeth, do you? Or comb your hair or put on your pants? Not usually.

There is no reason to forget daily maintenance tasks, either. Just put them in that same "muscle memory" compartment you use to drive to work each day. These are the things you do the minute you get there.

"If it's Tuesday, this must be Belgium," becomes "If it's Tuesday, I sharpen blades." End of story.

Two further points about maintenance. First, when you get a rain delay, it's great to take time off. But first be sure your machines are it top condition, parts and supplies are on hand or ordered, and so on. When it stops raining you might be very busy for a while.

Finally, it's worth buying spare air filters for all machines and spare blades for mowers. That way, when you're in a hurry, routine maintenance amounts to a quick change. The more time-consuming washing of filters and sharpening of blades can be done when you have time.

Repairs

Today's commercial turf machines are vastly superior to the ones we cussed at years ago. The dealers who sell them offer extraordinary levels of support, too: Parts are available overnight and contractors get "next on the bench" privilege. As a result, repairs these days are quick and easy, and lengthy downtime largely a thing of the past.

But of course dealers cost money.

You can save a lot of that money by doing your own repairs. (See Support for information sources.)

At the very least, on your daily rounds carry along tools and commonly-needed items such as spark plugs, belts, belt dressing, and starter fluid.

You'll soon discover that each machine, like each person, has its own idiosyncracies. Carry what's needed to keep each one happy.

But you can go much farther.

Doing your own repair work saves time and money, but mechanical knowledge is needed. If you misspent your youth as I did, patching up junk cars with chewing gum and baling wire, mowers are pieces of cake.

If you lack that experience, check the owner's manual, and go the library or look at online retailers. (Amazon lists hundreds of titles under "small engine repair.") Also check with local high schools and community colleges to see if they offer a course in small engine repair.

Big outfits commonly have full-scale maintenance shops, with compressors, welders, grinders, and lots of other power tools — plus mechanics to use them. Such a shop not only saves money but sets you free. When something breaks, parts are on your shelf; when it cracks you weld it back together now. No more waiting for parts to arrive from Seattle, no more panicky 6:00 PM races to the welding shop.

If you choose to do your own repairs, be aware that mowers are not like, say, Buicks. Buicks use mostly Buick parts. Commercial mowers have no such requirement.

Many parts can be welded or fabricated, and those that can't — engines, pumps, hoses, belts, pulleys, spindles, bearings, cables, chains, sprockets — are nearly always generic. This is standard, off-the-shelf stuff, with wide-ranging commercial and industrial applications.

It can be bought at a variety of outlets for a fraction of what you'd pay in a mower shop. But there's a cost here, too. Tracking down parts and doing your own repairs takes time — time that might be spent more profitably elsewhere.

In the end, you pays your money and you takes your choice. I've seen highly successful outfits that are heavily dependent on mower shops and others that are largely self-reliant.

See sample typical maintenance schedule on next page.

Typical Maintenance Schedule

Hustler ZTR	
Air filter – daily	6-1, 6-3, 6-4, 6-8, 6-10, 6-11
Oil & filtler – wkly	6-1, 6-8
Lube – wkly	6-1, 6-8
Blades – bi-wkly	6-1, 6-4, 6-8
Exmark 36	
Air filter – daily	6-1, 6-3, 6-4, 6-8, 6-10, 6-11
Oil & filtler – wkly	6-1, 6-8,
Lube – wkly	6-1, 6-8
Blades – bi-wkly	6-1, 6-4, 6-8
Edger	
Air filter – daily	6-1, 6-3, 6-4, 6-8, 6-10, 6-11
Oil & filter – monthly	6-1, 6-8,
Weedeater	
Air filter – daily	6-1, 6-3, 6-4, 6-8, 6-10, 6-11
Blower	
Air filter – daily	6-1, 6-3, 6-4, 6-8, 6-10, 6-11

Appendix

In the early 1980's we distributed 4,500 copies of the flyer below in upscale subdivisions inhabited by business and professional people. Prices on the flyer were low.

The first- week response was nearly $900 per week in new business. The flyer continued to pull for several years.

Let Us Keep Your Lawn
Looking Extra-sharp this Season

We specialize in the manicured look, and this year we're doing it at prices every homeowner can afford.

Check these prices for typical area lots:

60 X 120.......................

80 X 160.......................

100 X 220.....................

100 X 330.....................

Includes complete mowing, trimming, edging, and blower-cleaning of walks and driveway.

Grass clippings bagged and hauled away.

Additional Services Available

Free Estimates

Adams Mowing

419–866–5555

Call *Today* for these Special Spring Prices!

When I shifted from a crew operation to a tractor-only, high-efficiency operation, I needed more open, easy, "tractor" jobs. The ad below was run in a shoppers' paper distributed free in a broad swath down the west side of Toledo, where lawns commonly run two to ten acres. I don't remember the exact results, but only that they were satisfactory. The low price was reserved for super-easy lawns of five or more acres.

Below is a very simple proposal form, useful when you're just starting out and offer fewer services, or for simple residential jobs.

For a more detailed form, appropriate for a larger menu of services or larger jobs, see next page. Many more examples may be found online and at office supply stores. I suggest using a proposal form for all bids, both residential and commercial.

PROPOSAL FROM ADAMS MOWING

Project Location:

Work to be Done:

Terms:

Proposed by

(Title, Signature, Date)

Accepted by:

(Title, Signature, Date)

ADAMS MOWING INC.
1234 5th Street. Toledo Ohio 43635

419-865–1234 .jim@promower.net

Proposal

Customer name:_____   Phone_____

Address_____   Date_____

Lawn Maintenance for 2007 Season	Weekly ____
Mowing Price* $_____ per occurence	BiWeekly ___

Spring Cleanup_____   Mulch Installation_____

Pressure Washing_____   Leaf Cleanup_____

Fertilizer and Weed Control (per application)	Price $_____
April: Crabgrass prevention, broadleaf control, slow release fertilizer:	Yes_____ No_____
June: Broadleaf weed control, slow release fertilizer	Yes_____ No_____
July: Grub control, slow release fertilizer:	Yes_____ No_____
Sept: Broadleaf control, slow release fertilizer	Yes_____ No_____
Oct: Winterize, slow release fertilizer	Yes_____ No_____

Signature: _____   Date_____

*Mowing specifications: Complete mowing and trimming of the lawn, plus blower- cleaning of paved areas, to accepted commercial standards. Grass clippings mulched into the lawn. Also includes monthly edging of driveways and planting beds. Mowing height 3 inches, plus or minus ¼ inch, according to weather conditions.

Beginners in the mowing business often collect their money after each job. That's fine. Who doesn't like cash pay every day? But of course these constant collections are both unprofessional and a huge drag on efficiency. It's better to use a monthly billing system.

Business bookkeeping is beyond the scope of this guide. But if the subject is foreign to you, here's a simple accounts receivable system you can put to work immediately.

The system has two parts. The first part is the accounts receivable (money people owe you) ledger — an accounting book, spiral notebook, loose leaf binder, or something similar. This is what one page (this one belonging to Mrs. Smith) looks like:

Accounts Receivable
Mrs. Smith 124 E. Harbor Rd. Toledo 5525
419-000-9985
Weekly mow & trim. No edging.

6-6	Lawn Maintenance	$55	
6-13	"	55	
6-20	"	55	
6-27	"	55	
7-1	Billed		
	Paid		$220
7-3	Lawn Maintenance	$55	
7-11	"	55	
	"		

Notice that the page contains complete contact information for one customer, plus any special instructions or notes. The entries are self-explanatory. At the end of each month the charges are totaled and the customer billed. When the check arrives from the customer, the amount is entered under "paid."

The second part of the accounts receivable system is the statement or bill sent to the customer promptly on the first of each month. Appropriate forms are available at office supply forms or you can make up your own. Note that entries on the statement are the same as those in the ledger.

Monthly Statement

To: Mrs. Smith
Date: July 1, 2010
Terms: Upon receipt

6-6	Lawn Maintenance	$55
6-13	"	55
6-20	"	55
6-27	"	55
Total		$220

Adams Mowing
123 4th Street
Toledo Ohio 43611

Support

Associations

Associated Landscape Contractors of America
www.alca.org

Engine Service Association
www.engineservice.com

Lawn and Garden Dealers Association
www.lgda.com

Outdoor Power Equipment Aftermarket Association
www.opeaa.org

Professional Lawn Care Association of America
www.plcaa.org

Snow and Ice Management Association
www.sima.org

Trade Publications

Grounds Maintenance
www.grounds-mag.com

Landscape Contractor Magazine
www.landscapeonline.com

Lawn & Landscape Magazine
www.lawnandlandscape.com

Lawn, Building & Landscape Hotline
www.lawnbuildingandlandscape.com

Power Equipment Trade Magazine
www.hattonbrown.com

Pro Magazine
www.promagazine.com

Turf Magazine
www.turfmagazine.com

Equipment, Supplies, and Tools

Mostly mowers ....

AEBI	www.aebi-us.com
Ariens Company	www.ariens.com
Bad Boy, Inc.	www.badboymowers.com
BEFCO	www.befco.com
Clipper Elite	www.clipperelite.com
Cub Cadet	www.cubcommercial.com
DewEze	www.deweze.com
Dixon Industries	www.dixon-ztr.com
Excel Industries	www.hustlerturfequipment.com
Exmark	www.exmark.com
Ferris Industries	www.ferrisindustries.com
Flex-Deck	www.flex-deck.com
Grass Packer	www.grasspacker.com
GrassCatchersUSA	www.grasscatchersusa.com
Grasshopper Co.	www.grasshoppermower.com
Gravely	www.gravely.com
Great Dane	www.greatdanemowers.com

Grower Equip. & Supply	www.growerequipment.com
Howard Price Turf Equipment	www.growerequipment.com
Ingersoll	www.ingersoll-inc.com
John Deere	www.deere.com
Kut-Kwik	www.kutkwick.com
Lastec	www.lastec.com
LESCO, Inc	www.lesco.com
Massey Ferguson	www.masseylawn.com
Simplicity	www.simplicitymfg.com
Snapper	www.snapper.com
Steiner	www.steinerturf.com
Toro	www.toro.com
Troy Bilt	www.troybilt.com
Woods Equip. Co.	www.woodsonline.com
YazooKees	www.yazookees.com
David Bynum Group (Mower Sulky)	www.db-group.net
Dixie Chopper	www.dixiechopper.com
Lawn-Boy	www.lawnboy.com
Scag Power Equipment	www.scag.com
Walker Manufacturing	www.walkermowers.com
Wright Manufacturing	www.wrightmfg.com

Mostly blowers, edgers, and trimmers…

Little Wonder	www.littlewonder.com
Billy Goat Industries	www.billygoat.com
Echo	www.echo-usa.com
Homelite	www.homelite.com
Husqvarna	www.husqvarna.com
RedMax	www.redmax.com
Selbro Inc.	www.selbro.com
Stihl	www.stihlusa.com
Shindaiwa	www.shindaiwa.com
Tanaka	www.tanakapowerequipment.com
Aero-Flex	www.aero-flex.com
Bubco, Inc.	www.bubco.com
Edgit Corporation	www.edgit.com
McCulloch North America	www.mccullochpower.com

www.ingramcontent.com/pod-product-compliance
Lightning Source LLC
Chambersburg PA
CBHW071858200326
41519CB00016B/4444